Book Four   **Health and Growth**

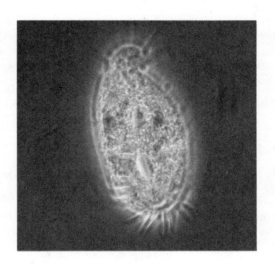

Julius B. Richmond, M.D.
Elenore T. Pounds, M.A.
Irma B. Fricke, R.N., M.S.
Dieter H. Sussdorf, Ph.D.

In consultation with
Orvis A. Harrelson, M.D., M.P.H.
Norman H. Olsen, D.D.S.
Wallace Ann Wesley, Hs.D.

Designed by Norman Perman
Anatomical Art by Lou Barlow, AMI

Scott, Foresman and Company

Authors

Julius B. Richmond, M.D. Professor
of Child Psychiatry and Human
Development, Harvard University;
Director, Judge Baker Guidance
Center; Chief of Psychiatric Service,
Children's Hospital, Medical Center;
Professor and Chairman, Department
of Social and Preventive Medicine,
Harvard Medical School.

Elenore T. Pounds, M.A. Writer;
lecturer; former Directing Editor,
Health and Personal Development
Program; classroom teacher; author
of *Drugs and Your Safety* and other
Health and Growth Enrichment Booklets.

Irma B. Fricke, R.N., M.S. Former
Director of School Nursing, Evanston
Public Schools, District 65, Evanston,
Illinois; recipient of the 1971
William A. Howe Award in school health.

Dieter H. Sussdorf, Ph.D. Associate
Professor of Microbiology and
Immunology, Cornell University
Medical College, New York, New York;
coauthor of *Methods in Immunology.*

Consultants

Orvis A. Harrelson, M.D., M.P.H.
Director of Health Services, Tacoma
Public Schools, Tacoma, Washington.

Norman H. Olsen, D.D.S. Chairman
of the Department of Pedodontics and
Dean of the Dental School, Northwestern
University, Chicago, Illinois.

Wallace Ann Wesley, Hs.D. Director,
Department of Health Education,
American Medical Association, Chicago,
Illinois.

ISBN: 0-673-04323-1

Copyright © 1974, 1971 Scott, Foresman and
Company, Glenview, Illinois. Philippines
Copyright 1974, 1971 Scott, Foresman and
Company. All Rights Reserved. Printed in
the United States of America.

Advisors

Grace Edwards, B.S. Fourth-grade teacher,
Morningside Elementary School, Salem, Oregon.

Thea Flaum, B.A. Former editor, *Safety Education,*
National Safety Council, Chicago, Illinois.

Willie D. Ford, Ph.D. Professor, Nutrition
and Home Economics, Grambling College,
Grambling, Louisiana.

Gladys Gardner Jenkins, M.A. Lecturer in
Education and Home Economics, University
of Iowa, Iowa City, Iowa; former member
National Advisory Council on Child Growth
and Human Development; author of *Helping
Children Reach Their Potential;* coauthor
of *These Are Your Children.*

Ruth Leverton, Ph.D. Science Advisor,
Agricultural Research Service, United States
Department of Agriculture, Washington, D.C.

Joan S. Tillotson, Ph.D. Consultant in
Movement Education; former teacher at
elementary through college levels.

Patricia P. Zakian, B.Ed. Fourth-grade teacher,
Lassen Elementary School, Los Angeles City
Schools, Los Angeles, California.

Health Editorial Staff

Thelma H. Erickson, Executive Editor; Terse
Stamos, Directing Editor; Jean Carr,
Associate Editor; Patricia Siegert and
Rosemary Peters, Assistant Editors.

Designer

Norman Perman, B.F.A. Graphic Designer,
Chicago; Guest Lecturer, University of
Illinois, Circle Campus, Chicago, Illinois;
past President, Society of Typographic Arts.

Regional offices of Scott, Foresman and Company
are located in Dallas, Texas; Glenview, Illinois;
Oakland, New Jersey; Palo Alto, California; Tucker,
Georgia; and Brighton, England.

Contents

1 What Are Some Wonders Of the Human Body?

Did you know that your body has many built-in ways of taking care of itself and of healing itself? Some of the body's special abilities include controlling its temperature, storing food and water for emergencies, healing cuts, and mending broken bones. These various abilities help protect us and keep all the body systems running smoothly. And the amazing brain ties all these actions together. You will learn more about these things in this unit.

1. How do you get the extra oxygen you need when you are exercising strenuously?

2. Are human beings warm-blooded or cold-blooded? Explain.

3. How does sleep refresh you?

4. What are some automatic actions of the body that help protect it?

5. What substances must your body have that are manufactured by the bones?

6. What reserve power does your body have?

How Does the Body Help Itself?

People often speak of the "wonders" of the human body. The body is also sometimes called "amazing." It has even been said to have a "wisdom of its own," because the organs carry on their work automatically. The body has the ability to help regulate its temperature, to store food and water for future use, to change food into forms it can use, to help protect itself, to summon an "army" to help fight off diseases, and so on.

Actually, it is very easy to find examples of the wonderful things the body can do. For example, as you sit reading this book, your heart is pumping blood round and round through your body.

When you are sitting quietly, your heart pumps about five pints of blood a minute through the body.

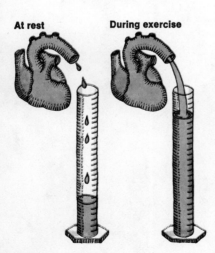

At rest   **During exercise**

When you run or jump or exercise hard, your heart pumps much more blood through your body than when you are at rest.

8

But suppose you go outdoors and have a race with your friends on the playground. As you run, your heart will speed up its work of pumping blood. It may pump as much as two gallons of blood a minute to bring your leg muscles the extra oxygen they need in strenuous exercise. This extra oxygen that the blood carries is needed by the muscle cells because of their contracting action during exercise. The action of the muscle cells also produces wastes, such as carbon dioxide, which must be carried away by the blood.

When you stop running, your heart will slow down its work. Very soon it will again be pumping about five pints of blood a minute.

All this happens without your having to think about it. Your body, in fact, carries on all kinds of important work every minute without your having to stop and think about it. Your heart beats; your lungs take in air and get rid of carbon dioxide; your stomach and other organs digest food. If you had to think about doing such things, you probably would not have time to sleep or to do much else.

Do you know some other ways in which the body takes care of itself or makes sure that it gets what it needs?

Your Body Helps Keep Itself at an Even Temperature

The body tries to keep the blood, which is flowing through it constantly, at an even temperature—a temperature of about 98.6° F.

When the day is hot—or when you are exercising and get very warm—you start to *perspire*. Drops of perspiration come to the surface of your skin

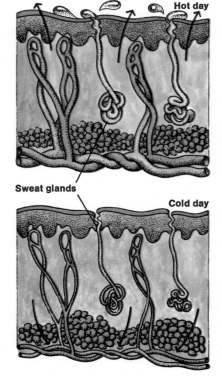

What does this picture tell you about how the skin helps regulate body temperature?

through openings called *pores.* As this perspiration evaporates, the body is cooled.

Also, when you get very warm, the blood vessels under your skin enlarge. This allows more warm blood to be brought to the skin surface, so that more body heat than usual is given off into the air.

When your body is too cool, the blood vessels under the skin *contract,* or get smaller. Then less blood comes to the skin and less heat is lost from the blood. Instead of the heat's being sent outside the body, it is saved to keep you warm.

Because the human body can keep itself at a comfortably warm temperature most of the time, people are called *warm-blooded.* Most animals, including birds, are also warm-blooded, although some animals like snakes and frogs are *cold-blooded.* That is, their bodies become cold if the temperature around them is low.

Your Body Makes Sure You Get Food and Water

Your body has ways of making sure that you do not forget to eat and drink. When your stomach is ready for food, its muscle walls begin to contract. This causes a slightly uncomfortable feeling and makes you think or say "I'm hungry."

When your body needs water, you have a feeling of thirst. Your mouth feels dry and your throat may burn or tickle. When your body lacks water, less *saliva* is produced in the salivary glands in your jaw. Then your throat becomes dry.

The sense of hunger and the sense of thirst are important reminders. You need both food and water to stay alive and to keep healthy. Food provides

What Do You Think?
What might happen if you did not have the senses of hunger and thirst?

10

the body's fuel, and water is needed for digestion of food, removal of wastes, and many other activities of the body.

Your Body Can Store Food and Water

Some of the water and food taken into your body each day is used at once; but some of the food is stored to be used as the body needs it.

Water is stored in the skin and in the muscles. And food that is not needed at once is changed into a form that can be stored until the time when it will be needed.

For example, some digested sugars are put away, as *glycogen,* for future use in the liver and to a lesser extent in the muscles. Some digested sugars may also be deposited as fat under the skin and around the organs.

This reserve supply of water and food is useful in an emergency such as during an illness. Another time when you may need reserve food supplies is when you are working hard or exercising strenuously. Then your blood picks up glycogen from the liver and carries it to the muscles of the arms or legs or wherever it is needed.

The food and water not used or stored for future use are moved out of your body. Some of the waste water is moved out as perspiration through the pores in your skin. Some is moved out through the *large intestine,* along with undigested or waste food. And some goes out with each breath. But most of the waste water is moved out through the *kidneys* and *urinary bladder.* And most of the waste food is moved out through the large intestine.

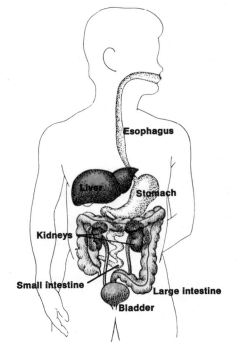

What organs do you see here that have to do with storing and getting rid of food?

11

Did you find these parts of the body in the drawing on page 11: *liver, kidneys, urinary bladder, large intestine?* What other important parts of the body are shown in this drawing?

Your Senses Help Keep You Safe

No doubt you know some of the ways in which your five main senses help keep you safe. What are these five senses?

Can you think of some ways in which the sense of seeing helps protect you? What dangers might your eyes help you avoid?

What examples can you think of in which each of the other main senses—hearing, smelling, tasting, touching—can help keep you safe?

You Sleep to Get the Rest You Need

All day long your senses send messages over the nerves to your brain. Your brain, in turn, sends back messages to your muscles. The muscles then do what the messages tell them to do.

By the end of the day both your brain and your muscles are tired. Then the brain starts to relax, and the muscles start to relax. If the conditions are right for sleep—the bedroom lights are turned out and it is quiet around you—you are likely to go to sleep.

As you sleep, the activity of your brain slows down, and your big muscles rest, though they may not relax completely. Your heart and lungs work more slowly, and this slowing down gives them a chance to rest, too. Because much of the body's work slows down during sleep, less energy is used and your body is helped to renew itself.

Normal brain waves during sleep

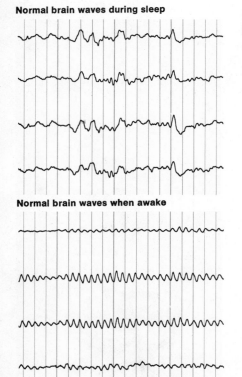

Normal brain waves when awake

Here you can see a record of the activity, or electrical currents, in a person's brain when he is asleep and when he is awake. These currents are called brain waves. The machine that records brain waves is called an electroencephalograph.

Sleep is an important protection for you. When you are growing, as you are now, your body has extra demands on it for energy. Sleep gives the nerve cells in your nervous system a chance to restore their energy and helps keep you from feeling tired and cross the next day.

Other Special Protective Actions

Many of your body's protective actions go on all the time, with no voluntary control needed; that is, they are *automatic.* If something comes near your eye, for example, you automatically blink. If a speck of dirt does get in your eye, tear glands in your eye send out tears to try to wash out the speck. When something gets into your windpipe, you begin to cough it up. If something irritates the inside of your nose, you sneeze. You touch something hot, and you automatically pull your hand away. All these actions happen without your thinking about them.

Still other automatic actions of the body show its special ways of protecting and taking care of itself.

Your eyes are able to regulate the amount of light that comes into them. When you are in a poor light, muscles in the *iris,* or colored part of your eye, cause the *pupil,* or opening in the iris, to become larger. This lets in *more* light. As more light enters the eye you can see better in a dark place. (See the drawing at the right.)

When you are in a very strong light, the pupils of your eyes become smaller to let in *less* light. Then you are able to see images more clearly. How

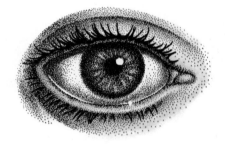

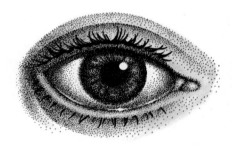

Which eye is receiving more light than the other?

13

might you check the changes in your pupils as you move from a light to a dark place?

Inside the nose are little hairs that help catch dirt and keep it from going into your lungs. The sticky fluid, called *mucus,* that is in the lining of your nose also helps catch some of the dust and dirt. The dust and dirt caught in the mucus are carried out when you blow your nose.

Your nose serves, too, as a kind of "air conditioner." As cold air passes over the folds of flesh inside your nose, the air is warmed. When warm air goes into your lungs, your body is kept from being chilled.

Inside your ears are wax and some little hairs. The hairs and the wax protect your ears by helping keep out dirt and insects.

The body is so designed that the food you eat goes down automatically when it reaches the back of your tongue. It goes down the food tube, or *esophagus,* into your stomach. When you swallow food, the roof of your mouth lifts back and covers the passage that leads to your nose. And a little gate of muscles closes off the passage to your windpipe. But when you breathe, the same gate of muscles stands open and air passes through the windpipe. Only once in a long while does any of your food "go down the wrong way." If, by chance, a little food does get into the windpipe, you usually cough it up quickly.

Food that is passing down the esophagus does not just drop down. The food is pushed along by the rhythmic action of rings of muscles in the

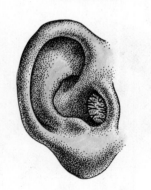

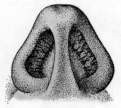

Can you see the protective hairs of the eyes, ears, and nose? What is their job?

walls of the esophagus. Because of this action, the food is kept moving in a one-way direction and a "back-up" is prevented.

Your Body Has Reserve Power

Some of the body's important organs come in pairs, such as the kidneys, lungs, eyes, and ears. Each of these organs provides what might be called *reserve power*. If one of the pair should be lost through an accident or operation, the other organ would use its reserve power to carry on much of the work once done by both organs.

For example, important as the kidneys are, a person can live with only one kidney. It is even possible to stay alive with only half a kidney, if that half is healthy.

If a lung should become diseased and have to be removed, a person can live without it. The remaining lung will do the work of both lungs, although the person may not be able to be as active as he or she was before.

If a person loses an eye, he or she can see with only one eye, although distance or speed of moving objects may not be judged as well as with both eyes. A person can also hear with one ear—even though he or she may not be able to locate the source of a sound as easily as before.

The body also has an amazing ability to *compensate* for, or make up for, various kinds of losses. For instance, if the eyesight is completely lost, the person may develop ability to use other senses to a fuller extent than he or she normally would. This ability in blind persons is well known. They

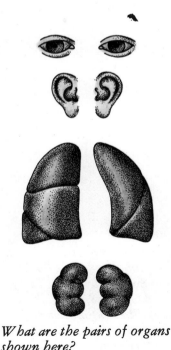

What are the pairs of organs shown here?

15

are able to find out about the world around them through their senses of hearing, touching, tasting, and smelling.

Your Body's Amazing Brain

The brain is sometimes called the busiest communication center in the world. It would be hard for you to imagine the huge number of messages that are sent to the brain continually. These messages are sent from the sense organs—the eyes, ears, nose, skin, and tongue. The messages travel over *sensory nerves.* Messages from each sense organ go to a special place on the outer cover of the brain.

For example, messages from the eyes go to the seeing, or *vision,* center, and messages from the ears go to the *hearing* center. Look at the picture on page 21. What other centers can you see?

Did you notice the *motor* center? It is from this center that messages go from the brain to the muscles telling them what actions to make, if any actions are needed.

The brain, spinal cord, and nerves make up the *nervous system.* (See the picture on page 23.)

One part of your nervous system takes care of all the actions you must think about and direct yourself—actions such as talking, reading, running, walking, singing, and writing. Another part of your nervous system takes care of the internal organs of the body. This part of the nervous system directs, automatically, all the actions that are for the good of the body as a whole.

Now study the pictures on pages 17 to 24 to learn more about the amazing human body.

Something to Do
A book that you may want to look for at the school or public library is Built to Survive *by Anne Terry White and Gerald S. Lietz (Garrard). Find out more wonders of the human body from this book or other ones.*

16

Some Wonders of the Human Body

If you could take off your outer layer of skin, you would see a layer of muscles and the bony skeleton.

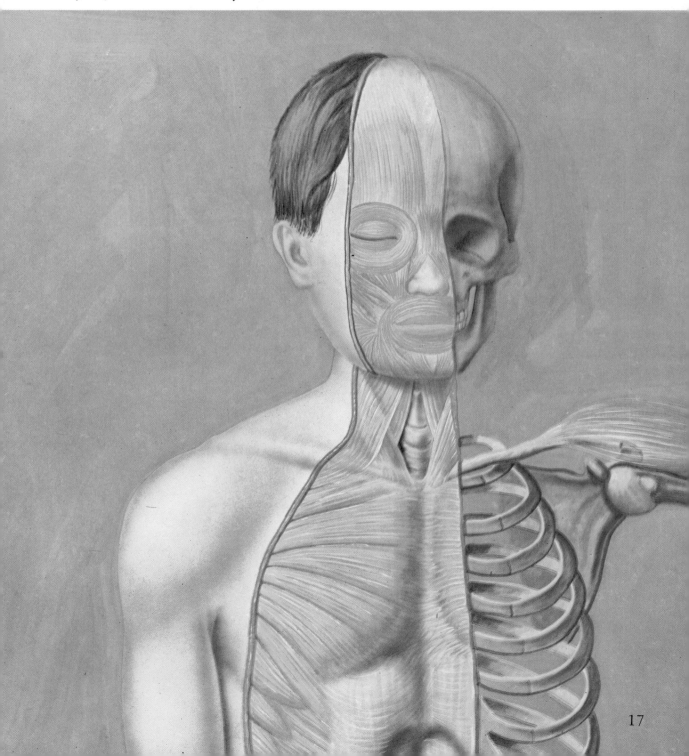

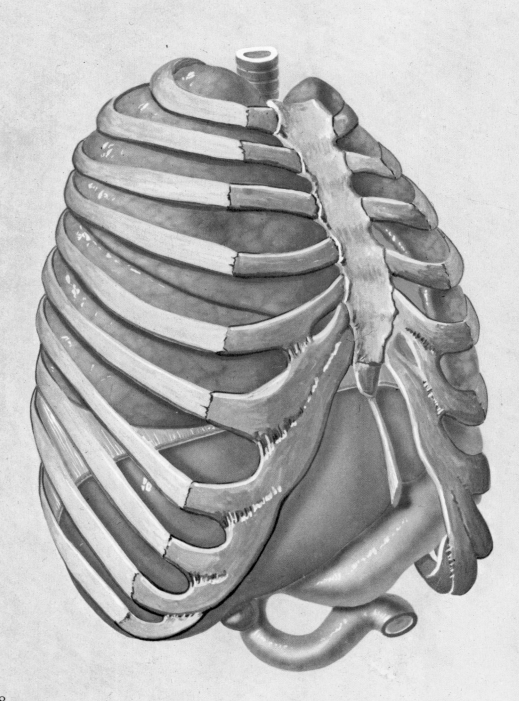

A remarkable thing about the human body is the way many organs are "packaged" in a small space. What are some organs you can see here?

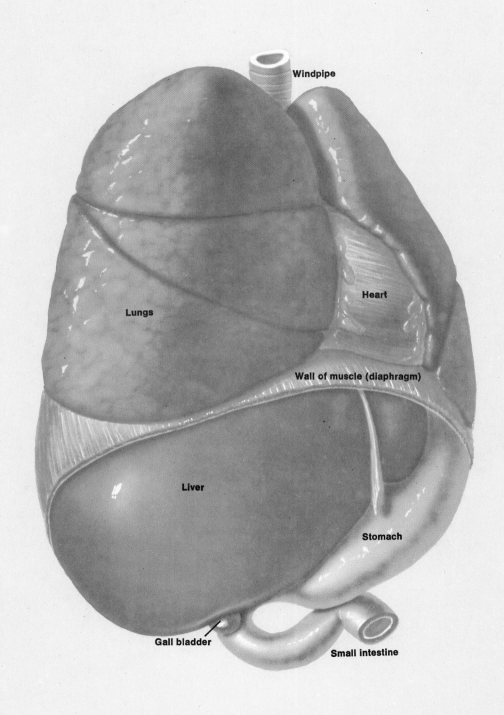

Windpipe

Heart

Lungs

Wall of muscle (diaphragm)

Liver

Stomach

Gall bladder

Small intestine

19

The skull bones protect the brain and allow for its growth. When you were a baby, there were wide gaps or soft spots between the bones. As you grow, the bones grow over and close these gaps.

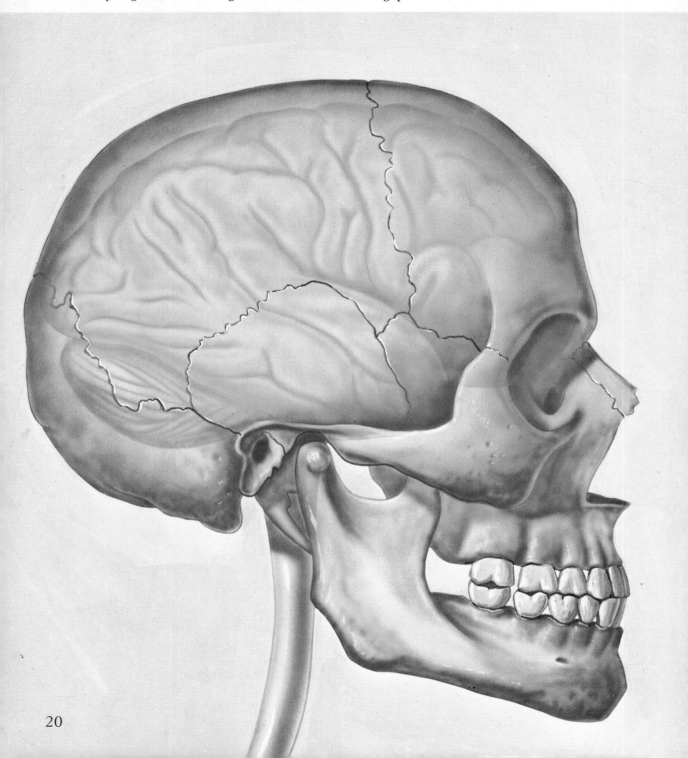

The amazing brain has charge of thought and memory, of movement and speech, of breathing, and of all other bodily functions; it keeps all parts working together.

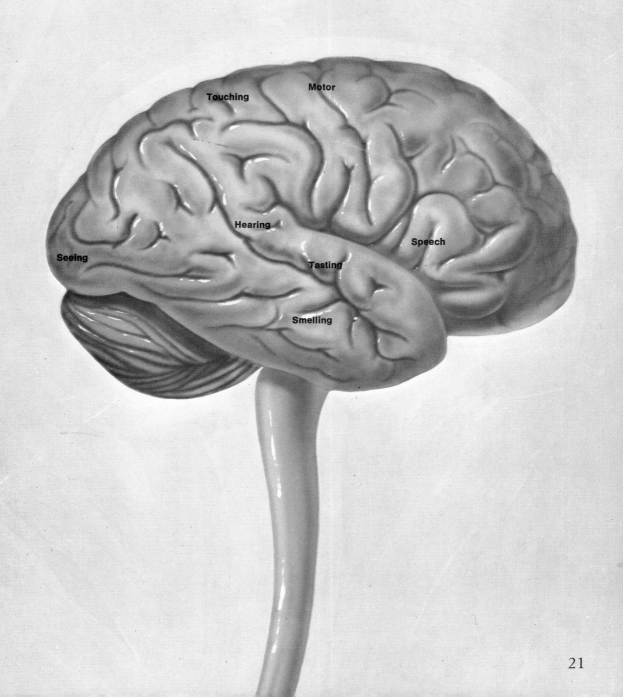

Another wonderful thing about the body is its amazing system of blood vessels. If these tubes were stretched end to end, they would circle the world about three times.

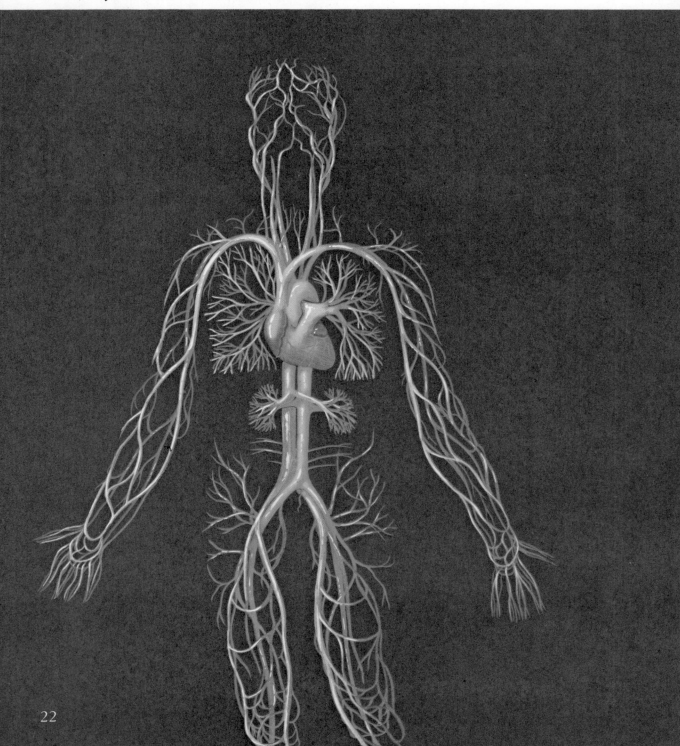

Here you can see the body's network of nerves. Did you
know that some nerves can send messages at a speed of
450 feet per second—more than three hundred miles an hour?

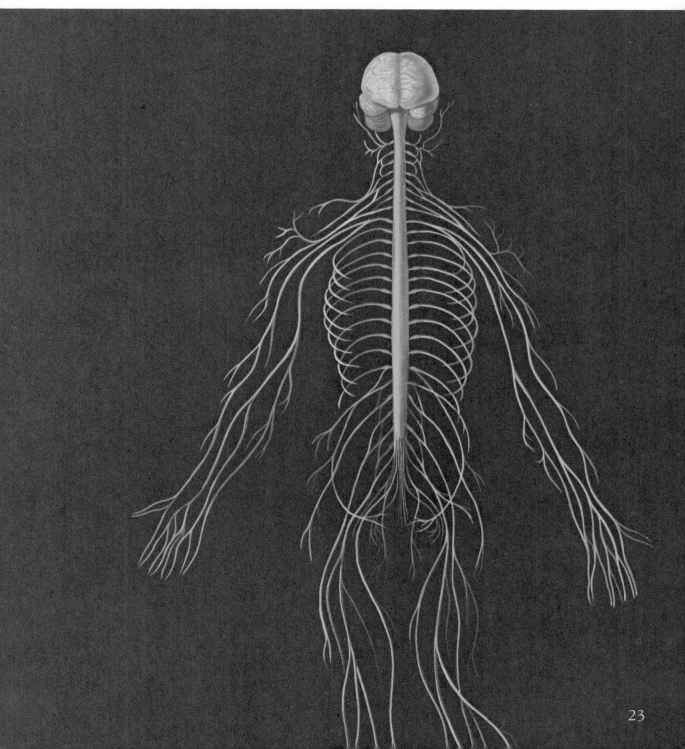

23

The hollow shaft in the center of long bones, such as the leg and arm bones, gives strength without adding weight to the body's framework. Red marrow in the ends of the bones manufactures red blood cells.

Health Questions Boys and Girls Often Ask

Here are some questions boys and girls your age sometimes ask about the body and how it helps take care of itself. Can you answer them?

1. How does a cut heal?
2. How does a broken bone mend?
3. Why doesn't water soak through the skin?
4. How does the body fight disease germs?

Check your answers with the ones below and on page 26. Then think of some questions *you* would like answered.

How Does a Cut Heal?

When a cut starts to heal, blood vessels in the skin contract to help stop the flow of blood. Tiny particles in the blood called *platelets* clump around the cut and then break up.

This action starts a series of chemical changes which cause the blood around the cut to thicken, or *clot*. The clotted blood fastens itself to the two sides of the cut. Blood can not flow past the clot, which hardens and forms a crust on the skin. The crust is often called a *scab*.

Underneath the scab, repair work goes on. The mass of clotted blood starts to shrink and this action pulls the sides of the cut together.

Later, cells of threadlike connective tissue enter the clot. These cells begin to build new tissue. Skin cells growing from each side of the cut join at the center of the cut. When everything is healed, the scab falls off. Sometimes there is a scar where the skin cells joined.

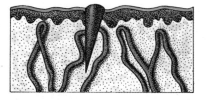

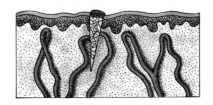

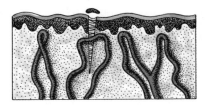

Use these drawings to help you tell the story of how a cut heals.

Sometimes, however, a cut is too deep for the body to heal by itself. Then the help of a doctor is needed.

How Does a Broken Bone Mend?

If you break a bone, the bone will heal itself. But unless the two ends of the broken bone are placed in correct position, the bone may not be straight when it heals. So the doctor *sets* the broken bone. That is, the doctor brings the parts together and positions them properly. After setting the bone, the doctor puts a plaster cast or splint around the break. This keeps the broken parts from moving out of place as the bone is healing.

As healing begins, each side of the broken bone makes new bone cells and pushes them to the other side. When they meet, the bone is healed. The healing may take anywhere from three weeks to a year or more, depending on how bad the break is and the age of the person. Older people's bones take longer to heal than those of young people.

Why Doesn't Water Soak Through the Skin?

Your skin has oil glands in it that send oil up to the skin surface. This oil covers the skin and waterproofs it so that water does not soak through it.

How Does the Body Fight Disease Germs?

If disease germs get inside your body, certain cells in your blood, the white blood cells, surround and destroy many of these germs. Your body also forms materials called *antibodies* that can fight and kill disease germs. The body forms a special kind of antibody to fight off each different kind of disease germ. You will learn more about the work of white blood cells and antibodies in Unit 7.

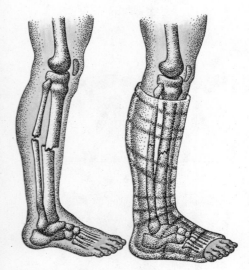

Here you can "look inside" a cast to see how it holds the broken bones in place until they heal.

26

Check Yourself

1. Look back at the questions on page 8. How would you answer them now?

2. What very important work does your body do without your thinking about it?

3. Where are food and water stored in the body?

4. What parts of the eyes protect them?

5. What happens when food "goes down the wrong way"? Why does this situation rarely happen?

6. How does a cut heal?

7. What makes your skin waterproof?

8. Why might the brain be called an amazing organ?

Something to Try

Feel your pulse at the wrist. Count the times the pulse beats in one minute while you are sitting.

Jump up and down 10 times and take your pulse again. What happens?

Things to Do

1. The class might make a booklet called "My Wonderful Body and How It Works." Volunteers might do research on any aspect of these areas. Museums could be visited or a doctor or school nurse might be asked to talk to the class as part of the project.

2. You might especially enjoy reading *The Question and Answer Book About the Human Body* by Ann McGovern (Random). See if you can find it in the library.

3. You have been reading about the many things your body can do to help itself —mostly things that go on automatically.

There are still other things you need to do to keep healthy and strong and to make sure you grow in the way that is right for you. Many of these things you have learned about in past years. You will learn more about some of them this year. Find out what they are by "reading" the picture puzzle on page 28.

One very important thing U

remember 2 do is 2 wash your

4 U eat and after U use the

Use some and warm

your th after U eat.

Or swish some around in your

2 wash away bits of food that

cling 2 the th.

Go 2 C the as often as

he th s U should.

Play out every day if U .

Do TV hour after hour.

Get some Xers instead.

sure 2 eat enough of the

right kinds of .

Go to in me 2 get

10 11 hours of sleep each night.

C your 4 regular health ups.

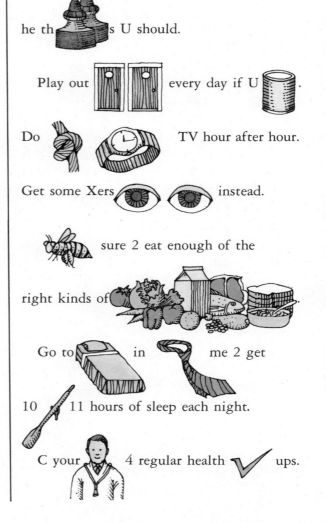

Self-Help Review

Use a ruler or a strip of paper to cover the answer column at the right. Read the first item and write the missing word or words on a piece of paper. Then move your ruler or paper strip down to uncover the answer and see if you are right. Go on in the same way with each of the other items. Do not write in this book.

The numbers by the answers show the pages in this book that give information about the subject. For the items you miss, go back and review this information.

1. Normal body temperature is about _____.

98.6°F. 9

2. When you are in a dark place, the pupils of your eyes become _____.

larger 13

3. When you exercise strenuously, your heart pumps blood _____ than usual.

faster 8,9

4. Your body stores water in the _____ and _____.

skin, muscles 11

5. Five important sense organs are the _____, _____, _____, _____, and _____.

eyes, ears, nose, tongue, skin 12

6. Messages from your sense organs such as the eyes and ears go to the _____.

brain 12

7. In your outer ears there are some little _____ and some _____ that help protect your ears.

hairs, wax 14

8. Disease germs in your body can be killed by _____ blood cells.

white 26

Copy each number on a piece of paper. After the number write *true* if the statement is correct. Write *false* if the statement is not correct.

1. Normal body temperature is 89.6° F.

2. Human beings are cold-blooded.

3. The body stores some food in a changed form in the liver.

4. Your heart and lungs slow down their work when you are asleep.

5. When you are in a strong light, the pupils of your eyes become smaller.

6. As the air passes through your nose, it is warmed.

7. If a speck of dirt comes near your eyes, you automatically open your eyes.

8. The food you eat goes down your windpipe into your lungs.

9. During strenuous exercise the heart speeds up to send an increased blood supply to the muscles.

10. When perspiration on your skin evaporates, your body is cooled.

11. Your body has no way of telling you that it needs water.

12. Most of the waste water in your body is moved out through the kidneys and urinary bladder.

13. The body has no need to store food and water.

14. The air you breathe in and the food you eat travel down the food tube.

15. The little hairs in your nose help catch dirt in the air you breathe.

16. If a bit of food gets in your windpipe, you cough it up.

17. Food is digested in the body without your having to think about it.

18. You have to remember to breathe.

19. Your eyelashes help keep dirt from getting into your eyes.

20. Your body has many ways of taking care of itself and seeing that it gets what it needs.

Number of Answers   20

Number Right   _____

Score (Number Right × 5)   _____

2 How Do You Grow?

The material in this unit will help you find answers to many of your questions about how you grow up physically. You will also learn about other ways of growing that are just as important as growing tall and weighing more. What do you suppose some of these ways are?

1. *Is there any weight chart that will show you* exactly *what you should weigh and how tall you should be for your age? Explain.*

2. *What can you do to help yourself grow in the way that is right for you?*

3. *At what age do many girls start to grow rapidly? At what age do many boys start their rapid growth?*

4. *What does it mean to "grow as a person"?*

5. *How can you become a better family member?*

6. *What feelings and attitudes can help you get along with others?*

7. *What are some advantages of the individual differences in people?*

Your head doubles in size from the time you are a baby until the time you are fully grown.
Your trunk grows three times its original size.
Your legs grow in length almost five times their original size.

How Do Nine- to Ten-Year-Olds Grow?

Do you ever find yourself wondering whether you are as tall as you ought to be or whether you weigh what you should? Did you ever think about how the *proportions* of your body change as you grow? If so, you will find some information in this unit of special interest to you.

For one thing, you may have the idea that you can find a chart that will tell you *exactly* how tall you should be and how much you should weigh at your age. But there is no chart that can give you such exact information.

You see, each boy and girl grows in his or her own way; each has his or her own timetable for growing. Some boys and girls your age may not be growing much for a while now. Others may be early growers and may be starting to "shoot up" and to gain weight.

Then, too, young people differ in body builds. Some children are short and thin, some are short and stocky, some are tall and stocky, some are tall and thin. Just by looking around you, you can see these differences in body builds.

The healthy nine- and ten-year-old girls shown on page 36 range widely in weight. And they vary in height over several inches. These ranges are normal for nine- and ten-year-old girls.

The nine- and ten-year-old boys shown on page 37 vary widely in weight. They also vary widely in height. Yet all these boys are healthy and growing in the way that is right for them. The ranges indicated in height and weight are normal for nine- and ten-year-old boys.

In thinking about these ranges, you have to keep body builds in mind. Thus a tall stocky boy or girl is apt to weigh more than a tall thin one. A short thin boy or girl will usually weigh less than a short stocky one, and so on.

Sometimes, of course, boys and girls may weigh less or may weigh more than is right for them. This may result from their not being able or willing to use what is known today about how to keep healthy. Generally, though, if it is possible for you to get enough of the right kinds of foods—but not

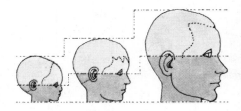

Notice how the head changes from babyhood to adulthood.

33

too much—and if you get enough sleep, rest, and exercise, you will grow in the way that is right for *you*. But always you must expect to find great differences in height and weight among those who are your age or close to it.

Sometime around the ages of nine or ten or so, you will discover something else about growth. During these years some girls start growing taller and making greater gains in weight than boys their age do. You might find a number of girls between the ages of nine or ten to thirteen or so who are taller than boys their age.

The picture chart on pages 38 and 39 gives you more information about how boys and girls do their growing. What does this chart show?

Remember, though, that not *all* boys and not *all* girls grow in these ways. Some boys and girls are fairly tall or short at all ages. Some young people grow up faster, and some more slowly, than this chart shows. The chart *does* show some general growth patterns, though, for boys and girls from ages five to seventeen.

There is one thing you can be fairly sure about. When boys and girls at last reach their adult growth in height, their bodies will be in proportion.

At full growth, your head will have doubled in size from babyhood. Your trunk, at adulthood, will have increased in length about three times its original size. When you are fully grown, your legs will have increased in length almost five times their original size.

Did You Know?
In the full-grown body, the arm is about three times as long as the hand—and the leg is about three times as long as the foot.

Individual Differences

If everyone in your group looked exactly alike, you might see a startling scene like this—with every face alike. How do you like it? On page 40, you will see a different scene.

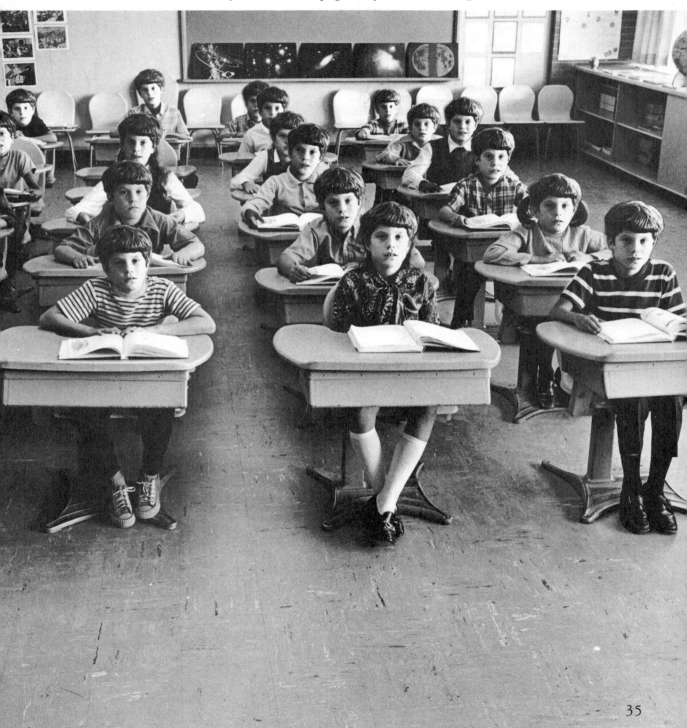

One of the many ways in which individuals differ is in height and weight. What are the ranges in height and weight for nine-year-old and ten-year-old boys and girls?

Nine-year-old girls
Height range: 48 to 57 inches
Weight range: 48 to 91 pounds

Ten-year-old girls
Height range: 50 to 60 inches
Weight range: 50 to 100 pounds

Nine-year-old boys
Height range: 49 to 58 inches
Weight range: 50 to 91 pounds

Ten-year-old boys
Height range: 51 to 60 inches
Weight range: 55 to 102 pounds

37

Below you can see and read about some general growth patterns for boys and girls five to seventeen years of age or so. What do you find out about how boys and girls usually grow up?

At five years of age, boys and girls are usually about the same height.

From five to nine or ten, the boys may be a little taller than the girls their age.

Around eleven or so, there may be a number of girls who are taller than the boys in their class.

At thirteen or so, boys are usually taller. After this age, girls grow some, but not a lot. Boys keep growing until seventeen or older.

39

Look back at the picture on page 35. Now look again at the
picture below. What makes this scene more interesting? How
would you explain some advantages of differences among people?

How Can You Grow As a Person?

You know that there is little you can do to *make* yourself grow tall. But it is possible for any one of us to make ourselves grow in other ways. These ways have nothing to do with height or weight. Each one of us can try to help himself or herself grow *as a person.*

For example, you can develop curiosity about things and can try to be informed about what is taking place in the world around you. One reason why schools exist is to help you do this. Today, people do not have to make up fanciful things to explain what causes rain and thunder and lightning—as people in early days did. At school you can find out scientific reasons for things that happen in the world around you. At school you can learn how to look up information you want and do not have. You probably realize that no one will ever know everything; but you find that you can keep on learning things and growing as a person as long as you live.

You can grow in skills and in the ability to do more things on your own. What are some things you can do to become more independent?

In the section that follows, you will learn still other ways of growing as a person. You will find out ways you can grow *in being a good family member, in learning to handle troublesome feelings, in showing kindliness and friendliness to others, and in being willing to appreciate the differences in other people.*

Something to Think About
Another way to grow as a person is in making wise decisions about safe or healthful things to do. For example, you can learn the facts about the effects of smoking or glue-sniffing. You can let the facts guide you in making your decisions instead of being influenced by what others do.
In what other ways might you grow as a person?

How Can You Grow As a Family Member?

Sometimes it is said that a good family member "carries his or her own weight." What do you think that means?

Now that you are nine years old or more, you will find that you can do many new kinds of jobs to help out at home. What are some of these new jobs that you are becoming responsible enough to do? Your class might make a list of the different ways all of you share in the work at home.

You can be sure you are on the way to becoming a good family member if you go ahead and do jobs such as these without having to be told to do them time after time. In the material that follows, you will learn of other ways in which you can work toward being a good family member.

Getting Along with Brothers and Sisters

There probably never was a family in which the children did not quarrel. Quarreling does not mean that brothers and sisters do not like each other. We all know that people who like each other very much may quarrel now and then.

However, if there is too much quarreling, it spoils things at home. And there are things that can be done to end or prevent some of the quarrels among brothers and sisters. Sometimes a quarrel can be avoided or ended if a child offers to take turns or to coöperate in a project or to share.

Another thing that helps avoid quarrels is getting enough sleep most of the time. When you are overtired, you are often apt to become quarrelsome.

WHY DO I HAVE TO WORK WHEN HE CAN PLAY?

Quarrels in a family may get started, too, just before supper when everyone is hungry. If there is a good TV program then, watching it may keep children too busy to quarrel. Also, having something to eat after school, such as a piece of fruit, can keep boys and girls from getting so hungry that they become cross before supper.

Quarrels between an older child and a younger one often start because the young one has been getting into the other's belongings. It helps when an older child's belongings are put away in a place where young children cannot get them.

If a person is very upset or angry over something, it sometimes helps to try to stay out of the way of brothers and sisters until there has been a cooling-off period. Then a fight will not get started just because someone is feeling mean.

On the other hand, it might sometimes help the person who is upset or angry to explain at once why he feels as he does. This may make him feel better and may help others see his side.

There are many times when one of the older children in the family can try to prevent a quarrel—or to end it before it gets worse. Just being willing to say "I'm sorry" or "I didn't really mean it" or "Let's make up" may help do this.

THERE HE IS, PLAYING WITH MY MODELS AGAIN!

Sometimes a quarrel may help bring hidden grievances into the open so that something can be done about them. Maybe one family member has been borrowing clothes or other things from a brother or sister without asking. A quarrel may help the borrower see that he must not do this.

Can you think of another example of how an occasional quarrel might have some good results?

Handling Jealous Feelings

Some jealousy is bound to exist among brothers and sisters in a family. Each child at times would like to be the only child and have all his parents' love and attention.

Jealous feelings may lead to angry feelings. If you often find yourself teasing, bullying, bossing, or bragging to a brother or sister, it is a good idea to stop and ask yourself why you are acting this way. Once you can understand and admit that you may be jealous of a brother or sister, you can do something about your feelings.

If you think a brother or sister is getting too much attention, or is being given things when you are not, it may help to remember times when *you* were favored.

I THINK MOTHER LIKES THE BABY MORE THAN SHE LIKES ME.

It helps, too, when you are feeling jealous if you try to understand the reasons why parents cannot treat all children alike all the time. For example, each child may require different things at different times. One boy or girl in the family may need a new pair of shoes, but the others may have shoes that are still usable. So the only sensible thing to do is to buy shoes for the one who needs them. Sooner or later, though, things are "evened up."

Children Have Different Needs

Children may not all be treated just the same because of age differences. People *do* seem to make more fuss over babies and young children than they do over older children. This does not mean, though, that they care less for the older children.

Furthermore, the ages of different children in the family account for what parents expect in the way of household help. You, for instance, are old enough to do a good job of picking up your things. Such help could not be expected of children who are much younger.

Since children in the family are different, you can see that it is difficult—and at times impossible—for parents to treat each child the same way.

You would not really like it if your parents *did* treat all of the children in your family just alike. For example, you would not want to have the same bedtime as a three-year-old brother or sister.

When you stop to think about it, fairness requires that each child in the family be treated according to his or her own special age and needs.

Meeting one child's needs at the moment does not mean giving greater love to that child. There is usually enough love in the family to go around.

WHY DO I HAVE TO GO TO BED WHEN SHE CAN STAY UP?

If you are an older child, you can see that it is only fair that you help at home more than do younger children. It can make you feel good, too, to know that your parents need you and depend upon your help.

If you have older brothers and sisters and are sometimes angry about the privileges they have, it helps to realize that when you are older, you, too, will have these privileges.

There is also the matter of individual differences in talents or abilities and in temperaments in the same family. One of the girls, for example, may be very musical and show real talent for playing the piano. So her parents may arrange for her to take piano lessons. Her brother, on the other hand, might not be interested in playing the piano; he might even be unhappy if he had to take piano lessons in order to be treated just like his sister.

Sometimes one boy or girl in the family has difficulty with spelling or mathematics. So, after supper, Mother or Father may take time to go over schoolwork with this youngster. Other children in the family, however, might dislike having special help with schoolwork just because one child is getting that help.

One youngster in the family may be very tidy and hate to have things out of place. This person may keep his or her part of the closet and special cupboards or shelves in very good order most of the time. Other children in the family might feel they were being treated unfairly if their parents expected them to be just as neat as this tidy boy or girl.

If you stop to think about it, there are many advantages in having your parents treat you as the very special person you are—and *not* just as they treat other children in the family who differ from you in many ways.

Then, too, there are advantages *and* disadvantages in any particular place in the family. What might be the advantages—and disadvantages—of being the oldest child? A middle child? The youngest child? An only child?

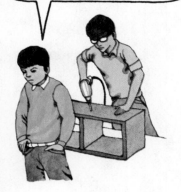

WHEN IS DAD EVER GOING TO LET ME USE THE POWER TOOLS? FRANK CAN USE THEM, BUT I CAN'T.

How Can You Grow in Kindliness?

Maybe you would like to grow in knowing how to get along with others.

One of the best guides is to *try to treat others as you yourself would like to be treated.* Another good idea, as is often advised, is to try to "put yourself in the other person's place." Doing so may help you look at a situation from that person's point of view.

Sometimes the books you read can help you better understand the need for friendliness and kindliness. Through reading, you have many chances to put yourself in the place of the story characters and to see things from their points of view.

Look at the activity at the right. In the books suggested here, there is opportunity for one or more characters to treat others as they themselves would like to be treated.

Two other good books are *A Dog on Barkham Street* and *The Bully of Barkham Street* by Mary Stolz. In *A Dog on Barkham Street,* Martin does some things that make you feel annoyed at him. You may even feel, time after time, that you do not like him. You do not feel that way, though, when you read *The Bully of Barkham Street.* There you find out some of the reasons *why* Martin behaved as he did. For *The Bully of Barkham Street* retells many of the things that happened in *A Dog on Barkham Street.* This time, though, you see everything from Martin's side.

Something to Do
Look for books such as these in the school or public library— books in which one or more of the characters show kindliness toward others:

Bishop, Claire H. All Alone *(Viking).*

Clark, Ann Nolan. Paco's Miracle *(Farrar).*

De Angeli, Marguerite. Thee, Hannah! *(Doubleday).*

Nordstrom, Ursula. The Secret Language *(Harper).*

Perhaps you remember reading the book *Crow Boy* by Taro Yashima. If so, you had a good chance to feel what it is like to be lonely and shy. You may have thought of things, too, that could have been done to make the boy in the story feel more "at home" at school.

At times the characters in the books you read face problems about friendships. For example, in the book *The Janitor's Girl* by Frieda Friedman, Sue Langer had a problem. Her father's friend had a daughter, Magda, who had just come from overseas. Magda did not speak much English as yet. She was timid, and she hesitated to speak for fear others would laugh at her.

Below you can read a portion taken from this book.[1] Find out what Sue's problem was. Then suggest what Sue might do.

"I hope you are going to be nice to Magda," Sue's father said.

Sue didn't answer. She just couldn't picture introducing Magda to Cathy, Marilyn, and the other girls in the neighborhood. She had a feeling now that some of the girls were nice to *her* only because she was Cathy's friend. What would they think if she became friendly with pale, frightened Magda?

Now look at page 49 and compare your ideas with the ones some other boys and girls your age have mentioned.

What do you think of each of these ideas? Which of the young people show that they are growing as persons?

[1]From *The Janitor's Girl* by Frieda Friedman. Reprinted by permission of William Morrow and Company, Inc. Copyright © 1956 by Frieda Friedman.

What Do You Think?
It is often hard for a newcomer to a school or neighborhood to feel "at home." What can you do to help a newcomer? What can the newcomer do to help himself or herself?

"I don't think Sue needs to worry about what Cathy and the others would think about Magda. Instead Sue might treat Magda as she herself would like to be treated if *she* were feeling lonely and scared."

Susie

"Sue could play with Magda when her other friends weren't around."

Jane

"Sue could ask Cathy and the others to help make Magda feel 'at home.' The girls could walk to and from school with her and things like that."

John

"Sue might wait a while until Magda learns more English and then she could start being friend-ly to her."

Mike

"If I were Sue, I'd really try to get to know Magda. I'd ask her all about the country she came from. And maybe Magda would teach me some words in her language."

Cathy

49

How Can You Learn to Appreciate Differences?

In talking over the book *The Janitor's Girl,* you probably decided that Sue and her friends, Cathy and Marilyn, might miss a lot by not getting to know Magda as a person. Instead of being concerned because of Magda's being different, they should be able to appreciate these differences.

By being willing to work and play only with those we think are like ourselves, we may often miss a chance for an interesting friendship and enriching experiences.

Imagine what a dull world it would be if everyone looked alike and wore the same kinds of clothes

There is a wide choice of things that individuals can do within one field, such as the field of music.

and lived in the same kinds of houses and had the same kinds of abilities.

But, fortunately, we are not all alike in such things as appearance or ability.

All of us are fairly good at some things and not so good at others. We can each contribute in our own different ways to our families and to the various groups to which we belong. This makes each of us special and important.

It is a sure sign that we are growing as persons when we can accept and appreciate the differences among people. We are growing when we learn we must not expect to be just like others—any more than we expect them to be just like us.

But the world is full of many other activities suited to the needs of different individuals.

Check Yourself

1. Look back at the questions on page 32. How would you answer them now?

2. Think about the boys' weight ranges on page 36. Do you think a tall nine-year-old boy who weighs 40 pounds is apt to be all right as far as weight goes? Explain.

3. What do the weight ranges of the girls shown on page 36 suggest about a tall stocky nine-year-old girl who weighs 90 pounds?

4. Why do you have to consider body build when you think of weight ranges such as those shown on page 36?

5. Do *all* boys and girls grow in the ways the charts on pages 36 and 37 tell about? Explain.

6. What have you learned that can help keep quarrels with brothers and sisters from happening too often?

7. What is a good guide for helping improve the way you get along with others?

8. Why is it not possible for parents to treat all their children in exactly the same way?

Things to Do

1. Plan a skit in which friendliness is being shown to a newcomer at school. Later talk over the considerate actions that were shown.

2. Be ready to tell or write about someone you saw recently who showed friendliness or kindliness to another person.

3. Tell about some evidence you have that you are growing in weight and height.

4. Write about some evidence you have that you are growing in ways other than in height and weight.

5. For the reading table, collect some books that tell about a character who has grown "as a person." Two books of this kind are *"What Then, Raman?"* by Shirley Arora (Follett) and *Grover* by Vera and Bill Cleaver (Lippincott).

6. Bring to class books from the library that give boys and girls facts to help make wise decisions about such things as smoking or experimenting with drugs or alcoholic drinks.

Two good books are *Drugs and You* by Arnold Madison (Messner) and *About You and Smoking* by Norman W. Houser (Scott, Foresman).

Self-Help Review

Use a ruler or a strip of paper to cover the answer column at the right. Read the first item and write the missing word or words on a piece of paper. Then move your ruler or paper strip down to uncover the answer and see if you are right. Go on in the same way with each of the other items. Do not write in this book.

The number by the answers show the pages in this book that give information about the subject. For the items you miss, go back and review this information.

1. Each boy or girl has his or her _____ way of growing.

own 33

2. Around the age of nine or ten or so, both boys and girls vary widely in _____ and _____.

height
weight 34

3. Between the ages of nine or ten and thirteen or so, a number of _____ are taller than _____ their age.

girls
boys 34

4. You cannot make yourself grow tall, but you can help yourself grow as a _____ .

person 41

5. A good family member does his share of _____ around the house.

work 42

6. It helps in working and playing with others if you try to _____ them as you yourself like to be _____ .

treat,
treated 47

7. Life is made much more interesting because of the many _____ among people.

differences 50

Health Test for Unit Two

Part I

Copy each number on a piece of paper. After the number write the letter that goes with the *best* answer choice.

1. Each nine-year-old boy
a. should weigh 75 pounds
b. has his own way of growing
c. should be 49 inches tall
2. Around five years of age
a. boys are taller than girls
b. girls are taller than boys
c. boys and girls are about the same height
3. Around the age of eleven or so
a. girls may be taller than boys
b. boys may start to grow up faster than girls
c. neither boys nor girls grow much
4. It is possible for a person to
a. grow as tall as he wishes
b. grow as a person
c. grow exactly as his friends do
5. Boys may keep on growing tall
a. until they are twelve years old or so
b. until they are about twenty-five
c. until they are age seventeen or older

Part II

Copy each number on a piece of paper. After the number write the correct answer, *true* or *false.*

6. All nine-year-old girls weigh the same.
7. You should try to treat others as you would like to be treated.
8. All children grow in the same way.
9. You can make yourself grow taller.
10. Healthy nine-year-old girls weigh from 20 to 30 pounds.
11. Proper food helps you grow.
12. The world would be more interesting if everyone were alike.
13. People differ in body builds.
14. You can learn from a weight chart *exactly* what you should weigh.
15. Your head never grows in size.
16. Exercise can help you grow.
17. It helps to laugh at a newcomer.
18. You can often end a quarrel.
19. A good family member shares.
20. When you are tired, you may feel quarrelsome.

Number of Answers   __20__
Number Right   _____
Score (Number Right × 5)   _____

3 What Can Foods Do for You?

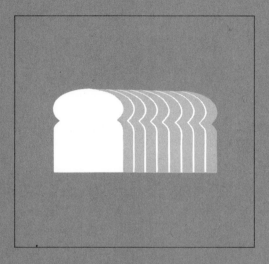

Does it really matter whether you
eat enough of the right kinds of
foods? In this unit you will find
out *why* it does matter. You will
find out what foods can do for you
and what can be done for foods to
make them appetizing and to keep
them from spoiling. You will discover
other things about food, too, such
as why lack of food is an
important problem in the world
today and what is being done to
solve this problem.

Read to Find Out

1. *What do the foods you eat do for you?*

2. *Why do you need different kinds of foods?*

3. *How can what you eat affect the way you feel?*

4. *How can you feel full and still be hungry?*

5. *How do you know when you are eating right?*

6. *What makes you get hungry?*

7. *What can make you lose your appetite?*

8. *What can cause food to spoil?*

9. *How can food be processed to help keep it from spoiling?*

10. *Why is hunger a world problem? What is being done about it?*

What Can the Right Foods Do for You?

Foods can do much for you if you eat enough of the right kinds every day, or at least most days.

The foods you eat each day have a great deal to do with how you *feel* throughout the day. For example, if you go without breakfast or if you eat a poor breakfast, you are likely to be cross and tired and hungry by midmorning. You may not want to do your classwork or listen to your teacher. Your body is telling you that it needs more nourishment to do its job well. On the other hand, an adequate breakfast can help you feel at your best and be able to work well during the morning.

Something to Do
Start now to look in your school library or public library for books about foods. One book you may find is The First Book of Food *by Ida Scheib (Watts). Others are* Plants That Feed the World *by Rose E. Frisch (Van Nostrand) and* Eating and Cooking Around the World: Fingers Before Forks *by Erick Berry (John Day).*

56

Of course, just eating *lots of food* will not take care of all the needs of your body. Unless you eat the *right kinds of foods* in the right amounts daily, you will not be getting the nourishment you need to keep you feeling your best and doing your best.

No single food can take care of all your needs. Different foods do different things for the body. For example, some foods are better than others for giving you energy. Foods rich in fat, such as bacon, butter or margarine, and nuts, are good energy foods. Other energy foods are "starchy" foods like bread, potatoes, rice, and grits. Foods with lots of sugar in them such as cookies and ice cream provide "quick energy." Some foods such as lean meats, eggs, and dried beans can help make strong muscles and help you grow in the way that is right for you. And still other foods, such as fruits and vegetables, milk, and fruit juices help keep your body working properly. You need water, too, to keep the body working as it should.

How do you *know* if you are getting enough of the right kinds of foods? Research workers have provided food guides that can help you plan a healthful diet. The "Food for Fitness" guide shown on pages 60 and 61 puts into four main groups all the important kinds of food needed each day.

What are the four main food groups in this food guide? How many servings of foods in each group does the guide suggest? What does the note at the bottom of page 61 tell you about water? What do you need in addition to *water* and the foods from the four groups?

How Food Helps You

Foods help make strong muscles.
Foods build and repair cells.
Foods keep you alive.
Foods help you grow.
Foods give you energy.
Foods help keep you warm.
Foods keep body organs working together.
Foods help you enjoy life.
Foods help keep you happy and alert.

How Can You Keep Food Records?

A good way to see if you are eating enough of the right kinds of food is to keep a food record. In this record you list all the foods you eat or drink during the day and the number of servings of each item. Be sure to include the snacks you eat.

It is a good idea to keep your food record for several days, because one day you might not eat so well as the next day. Also, you should not keep records of weekend or holiday meals, since these are not likely to be typical. Over a period of several days you can get a good idea of whether or not you are eating enough of the right foods.

A pattern you can follow is Ken's food record shown on page 59. How does this pattern help you check whether you have had enough of each of the four food groups? As you can see from the food record that Ken kept, you have to record what and how much you ate from *breakfast* to *bedtime*. Then you can tell if your day's diet gave you all the foods you needed in the right amounts.

Use the food guide on pages 60 and 61 to check Ken's record for Monday to see if he got enough of the right kinds of foods. Did he?

Remember that it is not necessary to have at every meal foods from each of the four groups in the daily food guide. But you should try to have all the suggested servings sometime during the day in regular meals and snacks.

Do you think that Ken's two snacks helped him get enough of the right kinds of foods? Explain.

Something to Do
Someone from the group might check with the school nurse to see if she has models of foods that could be used in assembling displays of a good day's diet.

58

Ken Perlo   Monday

For breakfast :
        2 servings browned potatoes
        1 fried egg
        1 cup tomato soup
For lunch (in school cafeteria):
        1 serving macaroni and cheese
        1 serving carrot and raisin salad
        1 glass milk
        1 orange
        2 molasses cookies
Snack between lunch and supper :
        1 apple
        1 slice bread with margarine
For supper
        2 servings chicken stew with vegetables
        2 slices bread and jam
        1 glass milk
        1 serving chocolate pudding
        1 peanut butter cookie
Snack between supper and bedtime :
        3 big pretzels
        1 cup cocoa made with milk

Servings   Group1   Group2   Group3   Group4
_____   _____   _____   _____   _____

Now *you* start keeping a food record for a few days. Check with the daily food guide to see if you have enough of the right kinds of foods from the four food groups each day.

Remember that your record is for your use alone. So keep it private. You may, however, want to talk it over with your family and explain what you are doing and why. Together you may think about and plan ways to improve your food choices—if that seems desirable.

Food for Fitness—A Daily Food Guide[1]

Milk Group: *Some milk for everyone*
Children under 9: 2 to 3 cups Children 9—12: 3 or more cups
Teen-agers: 4 or more cups   Adults: 2 or more cups

Vegetable-Fruit Group: *Four or more servings, including*
A citrus fruit or other fruit or vegetable for vitamin C

A dark-green or deep-yellow vegetable for vitamin A—at least every other day. Other vegetables and fruits.

[1]Adapted from Leaflet No. 424,
U.S. Department of Agriculture.

Meat Group: *Two or more servings*
Beef, veal, pork, lamb, poultry, fish, eggs
As alternates—dry beans, dry peas, nuts, peanut butter

Bread-Cereal Group: *Four or more servings*
Whole-grain, enriched, or restored

Plus other foods (see at right) as needed to complete meals and to provide additional food energy and other food values.

Other Foods

You will add to the four food groups some foods not specified— butter, margarine, other fats, oils, sugars, or unenriched grain products—to round out meals and satisfy the appetite.

You also need water to keep the body working properly. Five or six glasses a day, plus the fluids you get in milk, soup, and the like, are about the amount needed.

Why Is Lack of Food a World Problem?

In some parts of the world not enough food is grown to feed all the people. And often the foods that are grown do not have important minerals, vitamins, and proteins in them.

One reason for the lack of food is that the farmers in some of the developing countries still use age-old methods of farming. They do not yet have modern farm equipment, for one thing. And they are just beginning to learn about such modern methods as using chemicals to make crops grow better or to kill insects that destroy plants.

In some places the climate is such that there are long dry spells. There may be no rain for as long as two years. Such a long dry period kills the crops that have been planted.

Also some people live where there are no roads, so that food cannot be got from place to place, where and when it is needed.

Often, too, there is little or no refrigeration.

Under conditions like these, it is impossible for people to get the food they need. In some countries where there are many millions of people—even in years when the crops are good—there is still not enough food for everyone.

Some Ways of Solving the Food Problem

What is being done about the problem of hunger in the world? Our country and other countries frequently send millions of tons of food such as dried milk and wheat to help countries in need. But even more important, the

What Do You Think?
How do you act when you are hungry?
What could happen to a country that is full of hungry people?
Do you think there are any hunger problems in the United States? If so, why?

United States and other nations are helping the developing nations learn modern farming methods so that they can solve their own food problems.

How Scientists Are Helping

Scientists today are working to find new ways to solve the problem of hunger and lack of food. They are trying to make new types of foods out of things that are cheap and easy to get.

For example, there are millions and millions of tons of small marine life and great quantities of seaweed and other plants in the sea. So nutrition scientists are exploring ways to use these protein-rich products of the sea.

In recent years, a protein-rich flour has been developed. This flour, made from whole fish that is ground up and dried, has no fishy smell or taste. It can be added to ordinary foods to enrich them with protein.

Some other promising foods made of soybeans are the drinks, such as the one called Vitasoy, and chewy candy bars; both are enriched with soybean flour or other proteins. There are also chickenlike, fishlike, and meatlike products made of soybeans, such as those shown on pages 70-71.

Artificial, or *synthetic,* foods have been manufactured in some experimental food laboratories. Crude oil or petroleum has been used to make a tasteless, odorless white protein powder. This powder, in turn, has been used to make very good imitations of meat, chicken, and even cookies.

Almost any day now you may read in newspapers or magazines—or hear on radio or television—

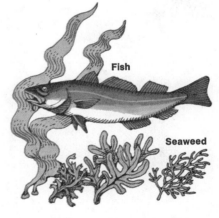

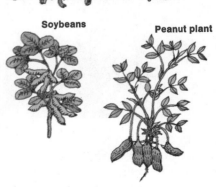

Some sources of protein-rich foods

about other new kinds of foods that scientists have developed to relieve food scarcity.

You will read about new *methods,* too, of making familiar foods like fish more easily available. For example, new devices have been invented to help fishing boats locate fish. Some of these devices shoot sound waves down into the water to help fishermen find large schools of fish.

Waters that have not been fished in very much, such as those around the Arctic and the Antarctic, will be explored more often. These areas offer some kinds of fish not very well known to most people but that are wholesome and that taste good.

Special "fish farms" may be set up where fish can be grown in scientific ways.

If water does not become too polluted, increased efforts will be made to harvest food from the sea.

Then, too, better kinds of seeds that can yield more and bigger crops are being developed in laboratories. In some parts of the world, this may be the most useful new step of all. For instance, a new kind of rice plant has been developed, a dwarf variety, that more than doubles the usual rice crop in Asia. This new kind of rice plant matures in about 100 days. Therefore a farmer could get two or more crops in a year instead of the usual number.

In some areas, it has been suggested, too, that substances be added to wheat flour to make the bread contain all the proteins needed in the diet.

On pages 65 to 72 you will learn more about world food problems and how they are being solved.

Fish and plants from the ocean may prove to be rich sources of food. However, water pollution may prevent this. Can you tell why?

64

Food Problems Around the World
*Food will be scarce in this East Indian woman's area
for quite some time. Can you tell why?*

These Philippine farmers are taking part in a rice-growing project. The purpose is to try out a high-yield seed that may produce greater quantities of rice per acre in a year.

66

In many developing countries the school helps improve diets and good health. The girls here will pass along to their families what they are learning about healthful foods at school.

67

Plants of a few basic kinds are an important source of food all over the world. Some of these plants, or foods that come from them, are shown below. What are they?

Banana

Coconut

White bread (wheat)

Rye bread (rye)

Potatoes

Sweet potato

Rice

Soybeans

Scientists today are working to make plants sturdier,
richer in nutrients such as protein, and able to produce
a higher yield than ever before.

Sugar beet

Sugar cane

Corn

Beans

69

To provide food for an ever growing world population, scientists are developing protein-rich foods. Soybeans are a good source for these new foods.

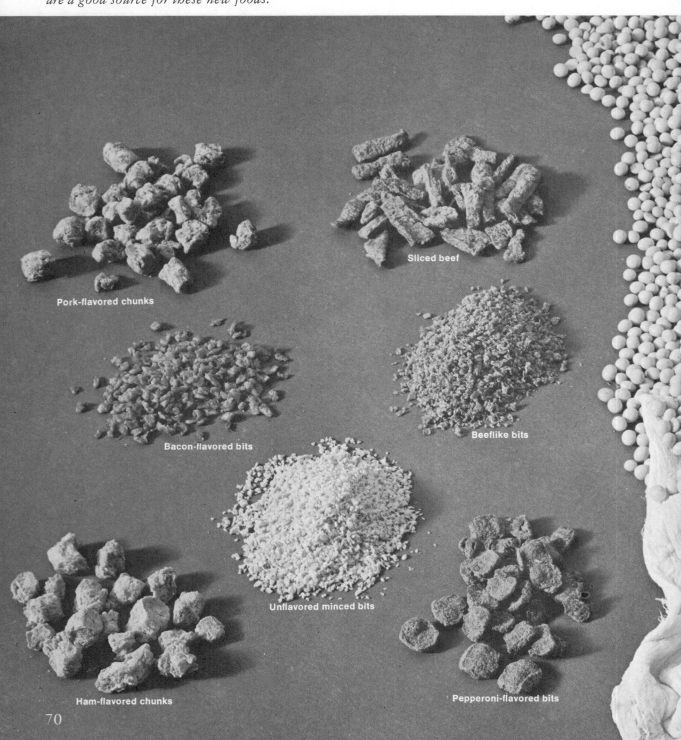

Pork-flavored chunks

Sliced beef

Bacon-flavored bits

Beeflike bits

Unflavored minced bits

Ham-flavored chunks

Pepperoni-flavored bits

Most of the soybean products shown here are flavored to resemble meat. When they are prepared according to directions, they can be used in sandwich fillings, stews, casseroles, and patties.

Soybeans

Unflavored bits

Beef-flavored chunks

Beef-flavored bits

Ham-flavored chunks

Bacon-flavored bits

Unflavored minced bits

Soybean fibers

7-1

Lack of food is a major problem in some countries. But in others, people must learn to select foods from a wealth of choices—otherwise they may be poorly nourished even though there is an abundance of food.

What Foods Do Astronauts Eat in Space?

In space, there is no *gravity pull*. This means that things float about if they are not fastened down. Foods are planned for astronauts with this fact in mind.

One answer to the problem of eating meals in space is bite-sized cubes that the astronaut places right in his mouth. These foods are softened by the saliva in the mouth. Some of the specially prepared bite-sized foods are brownies, sandwiches, toast, and fruit-cereal cubes. These cubes may be covered with gelatin or with a protein-and-oil coating. Such a coating prevents any crumbs from forming.

Other foods used on space flights are *freeze-dried* ones. These are foods that have been quickly frozen and then dried to lose their liquid and make them more compact. These foods include such things as orange juice, beef pot roast, roast turkey, and bacon and eggs. Such foods are treated so they will not float about and are put into plastic bags or tubes. When the astronaut is ready to eat them, he puts in water with a special water gun. In about fifteen minutes the foods are ready to be eaten from the plastic-bag "bowls" with a special spoon. Astronauts prefer the bag-and-spoon eating to the squeeze bags that were once used.

These foods that have now been developed will do very well on short space flights. But scientists are now at work on other types of foods for the longer space flights of the future. These foods must be ones that require very little storage space. Why?

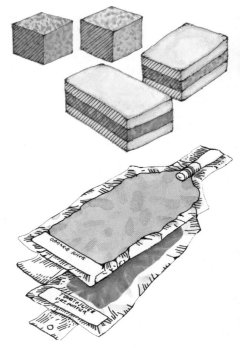

Research is providing ever better foods for astronauts. Some of these foods are now on the market for you to buy. What ones do you know about?

What Helps Make You Hungry?

You may have noticed that at times you are so hungry your stomach growls or even hurts a little. At such times you can hardly wait for your next meal. Now and then, though, you may have very little appetite. Why are you so hungry at some times but not at other times? Read on to find out.

Outdoor Play and Exercise

How do you feel after you have been playing outdoors for an hour or so? Usually you feel hungry, don't you?

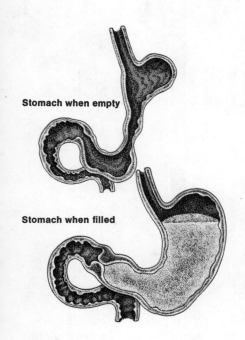

Stomach when empty

Stomach when filled

Work and play outdoors help your body use up the food you have eaten. Sitting quietly and reading or watching TV are activities that use up very little food. Sleeping also uses little food. That is why you can go all night without feeling the need to eat. When it is time for your next meal, your stomach may be empty or just about empty. Then the stomach muscles come together, or *contract*. This is the stomach's way of letting you know that it needs food. When the stomach muscles contract, you get what you call "hunger pangs."

Seeing and Smelling Food

Do you sometimes come into your house and *see* your mother fixing something you like for supper or *smell* some good food cooking? These sights and smells make you want to eat, don't they? Sometimes a person eats just because of the pleasant sight or smell of food, without actually being hungry. This is how some people become overweight.

Have you ever said, as you saw or smelled some food cooking, "That makes my mouth water"? You are right when you say that. That is just what happens.

Your *saliva* starts to flow and so your mouth really does "water." This saliva is a juice made by the *salivary glands.* The flow of saliva caused by the sight or smell of food is your mouth's way of letting you know it could start digesting the food you will eat. However, you may need to wait until the next meal to actually eat this delicious food.

As you chew, saliva from three sets of salivary glands mixes with your food and helps soften it so it is easy to swallow. Saliva also contains chemicals that change part of the starches in

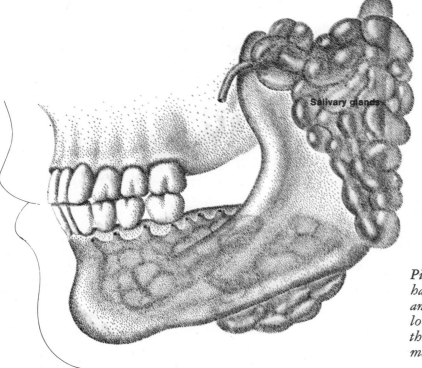

Salivary glands

Picture in your mind a big juicy hamburger with lots of mustard and catsup on it. How does it look? How does it smell? Does thinking about the hamburger make your mouth start to water?

the food you eat into sugars. These sugars can then be more easily dissolved and used by the body.

How Feelings Can Affect Your Appetite and Digestion

When are you most likely to have a healthy appetite—and when are you most likely to digest your food well? Is it when things are going well for you or when you are feeling upset?

You probably guessed. All your body systems work better, including your digestive system, when you are feeling good rather than when you are unhappy or angry or worried about things.

When you are unhappy, scared, or angry, the stomach does not do its work well. In some people, the work of the stomach is slowed down. In other people, the stomach works too fast. Some people "lose" their appetite when upset; others may eat too much, seeking some comfort from food. Over-eating can have serious consequences to a person's health.

When you are angry, worried, or upset, it is a good idea to talk things over with your mother, father, teacher, or someone else you like and trust. Do this well before mealtime if you can; then you are not so likely to come to the table feeling upset.

You can try, too, to help your family have fun at mealtimes. Talk about pleasant things that have happened, and try to avoid arguments. If everyone does this, all your family will feel more like eating, and their food will digest better.

What do you sometimes do to make mealtimes at your home more pleasant? Do you ever help make the table look pretty? What do you do?

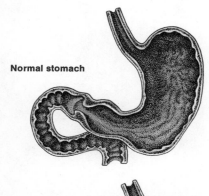

Normal stomach

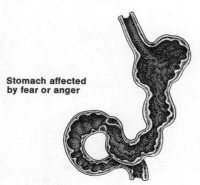

Stomach affected by fear or anger

Strong emotions such as anger and fear can cause a lack of appetite and can make it hard for food to be digested properly.

76

What Makes Food Spoil?

Have you ever gone to the breadbox to get a piece of bread only to discover that the bread had some spots of blackish or greenish mold on it? Or have you ever started to drink some milk and found that it did not taste or smell quite right?

In most cases like these, we say the food is spoiled. What causes food to spoil?

One important reason why many fresh foods spoil is that certain *microörganisms,* or *microbes,* get into them and grow. Microörganisms are tiny plants and animals that are found all around you —in the air, in the ground, in the water. They are on your hands and on your clothes. Everything you touch has microbes on it, but you cannot see them because they are so tiny.

Most of the microörganisms in the world around you will not harm you, and many of them are helpful. Some microörganisms help make changes in the ground so that plants grow well in it. Other microörganisms are used to make medicines. Still others are used to make pickles, bread, cheese.

The harmful microbes are those that cause foods to spoil and the ones that cause disease.

Bacteria, molds, and *yeasts* are some of the microorganisms that are most likely to get into foods and spoil them. Yeasts are sometimes used, though, in food preparation to make bread and rolls.

How do we know that harmful microbes have been at work in our foods and have spoiled them? It may be because of their strange smell or taste.

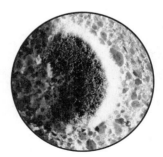

Here you can see a piece of bread that has been spoiled by mold.

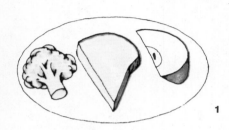

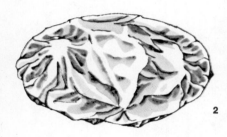

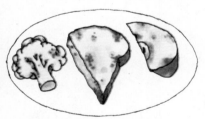

Something to Try
1. Put a piece of cooked vegetable, a piece of bread, and a piece of sliced fruit on a pie plate. Leave the food in the open air for an hour or so.
2. Cover the plate and put it in a warm, dark place. Look at the food each day.
3. When clumps of microbes appear, look at them under a magnifying glass or a microscope.

This happens because, as the microbes eat and digest the food, they produce wastes that cause an unpleasant odor or taste. The food may soon become covered with blackish or greenish mold. In the case of yeasts, a scum may form on liquid foods.

Sometimes, however, there may be no signs—either in the taste, smell, or appearance—that would indicate a food has spoiled.

Eating food that contains many harmful microorganisms can cause people to become sick.

How Foods Are Kept from Spoiling

To help keep foods from spoiling, we have to make sure that bacteria, molds, and yeasts do not grow in the foods. These microörganisms will not grow unless they have the things needed to encourage their growth, things like dampness and warmth. Most microbes grow best in warm but not *hot* places. And they grow very slowly in cold places.

That is why we try to keep foods that spoil easily, foods like milk, butter, eggs, meat, fish, and most fruits and vegetables, in a cold place such as a refrigerator or a freezer. Refrigeration *slows* bacteria growth, while freezing stops it. This keeps the foods from spoiling as quickly as they otherwise would.

Certain foods are especially apt to spoil in the summer if they are left in a warm place. We read fairly often in the newspapers about people who have become sick at picnics from eating foods that had started to spoil because they had not been kept cool. Foods such as custards, cream fillings in cakes and pies, salad dressings, rice, and cornbread stuffings spoil very easily in summer. Such foods should be kept refrigerated until they are to be eaten.

Leftover foods should also be refrigerated to keep them from spoiling. Frozen foods that have been thawed should not be refrozen.

To help keep bacteria out of foods and lessen their chance of spoiling and of making you sick, care must be taken in preparing foods, too. Microorganisms can get into foods by someone's coughing or sneezing on them. Also, touching foods with hands that are dirty or that have an open cut or sore on them can spread germs into the food. Storing foods properly is important, too. Foods like sugar and flour should be kept tightly covered to avoid the spread of disease by insects and other pests.

To make sure the foods you eat are safe, the local health department usually requires food-handlers in public places to have periodic health examinations. Often classes are given by public health workers to teach food-handlers the sanitary way to do things.

Workers from the public health department also check the cleanliness of food sold in grocery stores and in restaurants. Furthermore, dishwashing and table-setting methods are carefully checked to be sure that eating utensils do not have harmful bacteria on them.

Ways of Processing Food to Keep It from Spoiling

Since microörganisms cannot grow in dry places, one common method of keeping food from spoiling is to dry it.

Some Things to Find Out
1. If there is a lunchroom at your school, find out how foods are stored to help prevent them from spoiling.
2. Talk to someone you know who is a cook or a waitress or a manager of a restaurant. See what rules he or she follows for handling foods in sanitary ways.

Just think of all the foods at your house that are kept from spoiling because they have been dried—rice, flour, beans, prunes, powdered milk, raisins. Drying foods is a process that has been used over the centuries. Long ago most food was dried by putting it in the sun. Today food factories have special rooms and equipment for the rapid drying of foods.

Salt can help preserve food, also. And sometimes vinegar and spices are added to give the foods a taste that many people like. This is what is done with pickles and various spiced vegetables and fruits.

Think, too, about the foods that are bought in cans and jars. Sometimes these cans and jars of food are on the shelf for weeks or months before we open them. What has been done to keep the foods in them from spoiling? At the factory the cans or jars of food are cooked at high enough temperatures to kill any microbes that might be in the food. When the cans come out of the cookers, the food in them is *sterile,* or free from living microbes.

Foods can be frozen, too, and kept in a freezer for a long time without spoiling. What are some frozen foods you have eaten lately?

You learned earlier about the way of preserving foods known as *freeze-drying.* Fresh foods are quickly frozen and then dried to remove the liquid content. When they are cooked, water is restored, and they have their original fresh flavor. Some foods processed by this freeze-dry method have been kept unrefrigerated for years without spoiling.

Can you find these ways of preserving foods in the pictures above: Frozen? Pickled? Dried? Canned? Freeze-dried?

80

Health Questions Boys and Girls Often Ask

Is There Any Harm in Candy and Soft Drinks?

Most everyone enjoys sweets, and most people need moderate amounts in their diets. Sweets become harmful only if you let them take the place of important protective foods you need—or use them to add food energy you don't need.

Too much candy or too many soft drinks may spoil your appetite for the milk, bread and cereals, meat, and vegetables and fruits you need daily. You have probably found that out for yourself.

Sugar is the major ingredient in most soft drinks and in many candies. Therefore, these provide chiefly energy in the form of *calories.*

Sweets are commonly used as snack foods. Because snacks are an important part of your daily diet, they should provide some part of all the food nutrients you need every day. Fruits, juices, raw vegetable sticks, milk, and cereals are much better snack foods than sweets.

A good time for sweets is at the end of a meal. Then the sweets round out the meal and satisfy but do not spoil the appetite.

Your dentist may warn you, too, that sticky, sweet foods like candy help cause cavities in your teeth. Therefore you should brush your teeth after you have eaten sweets, if possible. Be *sure* to brush your teeth well at least once a day.

Should Boys and Girls Drink Tea and Coffee?

Tea and coffee have no food value, except for the little that is added if sugar and cream are

Something to Do
Notice the labels on cartons of cereal, on cans, and on containers of other foods. Look for what are called nutritional labels. Be ready to talk over the kinds of information given on nutritional labels. Bring some of the labels to class.

81

used or if lemon is put in the tea. There is practically nothing in these drinks to help you grow or help you stay well. One harm in using them is that they are likely to crowd out of your daily diet the milk you need.

Most brands of tea and coffee contain a small amount of the drug *caffeine.* This drug speeds up the work of the heart and can be harmful.

Do Alcoholic Drinks and Tobacco Hurt the Body?

Alcoholic drinks have an effect on the working of the brain. When people drink large amounts of such beverages as beer, wine, gin, and whiskey, they are not able to control their bodies or their behavior. Then they are more likely to become involved in accidents. Excessive use over a long period is harmful to an individual's health.

Smoking often spoils the appetite, and so smokers may not eat enough of the right kinds of foods. But a more serious danger is the fact that smoking may cause lung cancer. It is also believed to be a cause of many problems of the breathing and circulatory systems.

What Is Wrong with Eating in a Hurry?

If you do not chew your food well, it will be harder for your stomach to do its work. Digestion starts as you chew your food and saliva mixes with it. This makes the food easier to swallow and easier for the stomach to digest. Also, chewing food well gives the saliva time to start changing starch into sugar in such foods as bread and potatoes. Another danger in eating in a hurry is that sometimes you may eat more than you need.

Some Things to Do
1. Ask your school nurse or your parents what warning is put on every package of cigarettes. Be ready to tell about this warning.
2. Tell why people who drink large amounts of alcoholic beverages may have traffic accidents.
3. Look for information about the harmful things that are in cigarette smoke. The book About You and Smoking *by Norman Houser (Scott, Foresman) may help you. Or look in the encyclopedia.*
4. Tell why you think "ads" about cigarettes are no longer allowed on television.

Check Yourself

1. Look back at the questions on page 56. How would you answer them now?

2. How would you explain each of these terms?

   a. saliva

   b. salivary glands

   c. food guide

3. Which of the following activities would cause you to need extra energy food?

   a. watching TV

   b. playing ball

   c. resting in a chair

   d. jumping rope

4. Why do you need *different* kinds of foods each day?

5. What are the important food groups in the daily food guide?

6. Why do we store foods such as meat, fish, milk, eggs, and most fresh fruits and vegetables in the refrigerator?

7. Why do dried foods not spoil?

Things to Do

1. Write a paragraph about your favorite food. Be sure to tell some reasons why you like it.

2. Use the food guide pictured on pages 60 and 61 to check the day's menus shown below. Are enough of the right kinds of foods included in the meals and snacks for a single day?

Breakfast

2 servings grits

1 serving bacon

1 cup of cocoa
   made with milk

Lunch

1 cheese sandwich

1 orange

3 cookies

1 glass milk

Supper

2 servings spaghetti
   and meat balls

2 pieces of cornbread

1 serving beet greens

1 glass milk

1 piece cake

Snacks

3 cookies

1 candy bar

3. Tell or write about something you can cook for your family.

4. Sometimes you feel especially hungry when you are the one who has done the cooking. This is more apt to be true if you have had a chance to help choose what you are to cook.

A good way to begin as a cook is to try making some quick and easy snacks. For example, you can see pictured on this page some foods that might be used as snacks. What are these foods? How do you make each one?

Decide which of these foods *you* would like to try to make at home. Copy your favorite recipes carefully and take them home. Talk them over with your parents and, if possible, try to make them soon.

Hot Dogs in Biscuits

Package of prepared biscuit mix.

Enough hot dogs for the family

Make the biscuit dough as directed on the package. (Canned biscuits may also be used.) Roll the dough to a thickness of about 1/4 inch. Cut the dough into 4-inch squares. Wrap each square of dough around a hot dog, let the ends of the hot dog show. Bake 15 minutes in a 450° oven. Serve hot.

Quick Shake

1 cup cold milk

2 tablespoons of instant pudding mix, any flavor you wish.

Put the milk and pudding mix into a clean jar and screw on top of jar tightly. Shake well.

Cinnamon Toast

1 teaspoon of butter

1/4 teaspoon of cinnamon

1/2 teaspoon of sugar

1 slice of toast

Spread butter on a slice of toast. Sprinkle sugar and cinnamon over it.

Special Research

1. Pick a food such as a fresh fruit, a canned food, or a freeze-dried food. Prepare a report on how it is obtained, how it is processed, and how it gets to the store.

2. Investigate and report on the kinds of foods grown or processed in your community.

84

Self-Help Review

Use a ruler or a strip of paper to cover the answer column at the right. Read the first item and write the missing word or words on a piece of paper. Then move your ruler or paper strip down to uncover the answer and see if you are right. Go on in the same way with each of the other items. Do not write in this book.

The numbers by the answers show the pages in this book that give information about the subject. For the items you miss, go back and review this information.

1. In addition to eating foods from the _____ main food groups, you also need to drink _____ to keep your body working as it should.

four, water
57

2. Boys and girls your age need _____ or more cups of milk a day.

three 60-61

3. You need _____ or more servings from the vegetable-fruit group each day.

four 60-61

4. You need _____ or more servings from the bread-cereal group each day.

four 60-61

5. You need_____or more servings from the meat group each day.

two 60-61

6. When your mouth "waters," the _____ is beginning to flow.

saliva 75

7. When you are angry or worried or otherwise upset, you may not feel as_____as you usually do.

hungry 76

8. Microbes in foods stop growing—or grow very slowly—in _____ temperatures.

cold 78

9. Microbes in foods grow rapidly in _____ but not hot temperatures.

warm 78

Health Test for Unit Three

Copy each number on a piece of paper. After the number write the correct answer, *true* or *false*.

1. Outdoor play and exercise help your body use the food you have eaten.

2. Quarrels tend to make mealtimes unpleasant.

3. Saliva is another name for water.

4. Foods help you grow.

5. Alcoholic drinks keep the brain from doing its work properly.

6. All you need to know about food is that you should eat lots of it every day.

7. Tea and coffee are drinks that are very rich in protein.

8. A daily food guide tells us what kinds of foods and how much of them we should eat every day.

9. You should wash your hands before you cook or serve food.

10. Foods can give you energy.

11. You need just one cup of milk a day.

12. You need four or more servings from the vegetable-fruit group each day.

13. The only reason a food spoils is that it gets old and stale.

14. You need four or more servings of foods from the meat group each day.

15. Saliva starts to digest the starches in the food you eat.

16. Microbes grow fast in temperatures that are very hot.

17. Microbes grow slowly in temperatures that are very cold.

18. The smell of food cooking can make you hungry.

19. All the people in the world are able to get enough food to eat.

20. You can live without water.

Number of Answers   <u> 20 </u>

Number Right   <u>   </u>

Score (Number Right × 5)   <u>   </u>

4 How Much Do You Know About Your Teeth?

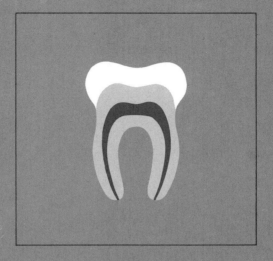

What are your teeth made of, and what important jobs do they do? How can teeth best be cared for? Are there any new things to be learned about care of the teeth? If so, what are they? These are some of the questions that will be answered in this unit.

Read to Find Out

1. *What are the parts of a tooth?*

2. *What are teeth made of?*

3. *What part of the tooth hurts when you have a toothache?*

4. *How are different-shaped teeth used?*

5. *What would happen if you had no teeth?*

6. *What can you do to help prevent tooth decay?*

7. *What research is being done on tooth care?*

What Are Teeth Made Of?

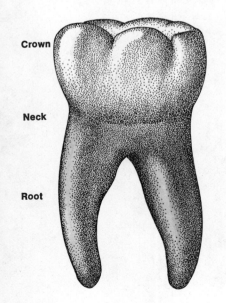

Crown

Neck

Root

You already know something about the different parts of a tooth. The part that you can see—and that you chew with—is the *crown.* Under the gums, where you cannot see them, are *roots.* Some teeth have only one root; others have two roots; still others have three roots. The crown and root, or roots, join at the *neck* of the tooth.

Each tooth is made of four different kinds of tissue—*enamel, cementum, dentin,* and *pulp.* (See the drawing on page 94.) The white covering of the crown is the *enamel.* This enamel is very hard —even harder than your bones. It has to be hard to protect the tooth from injury as you bite into and chew all kinds of foods. The enamel helps protect the inner parts of the tooth from the bacteria that cause decay. Once the enamel has been formed on a tooth, this enamel does not grow back if it is injured.

The covering of the root of the tooth is the bonelike tissue called *cementum.* The root is attached to the jawbone with elasticlike fibers. These fibers form what is called the *periodontal membrane.* This membrane enables the dentist to *extract,* or pull, a tooth without injuring the surrounding jawbone. The membrane also acts as a shock absorber to lessen the jarring caused by chewing.

The layer of tissue that is under the enamel and cementum is the hard bonelike material called *dentin.* Dentin makes up the biggest part of the tooth. When a cavity in a tooth spreads to the dentin, the nerves carry messages of pain to the brain. It is this part of the tooth that hurts when you have a toothache.

Within a hollow space in the center of the tooth is a soft mass of tissue called *pulp.* The pulp contains blood vessels and nerves. These enter the tooth through an opening in the root.

The pictures on page 95 show how decay can break through the enamel and then spread through a tooth and cause trouble. After you study these pictures, you will understand why you should visit your dentist as often as he advises.

The dentist will check your teeth for *dental caries,* or *cavities,* that need filling. The dentist will also check for *tartar,* or *calculus,* a hard yellow substance that forms on the surfaces of the teeth. Calculus can irritate your gums and make them bleed. Calculus can be removed with a special instrument called a *scaler.* Often a worker known as a *dental hygienist* cleans your teeth.

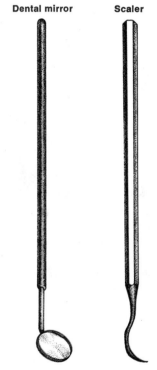

Dental mirror   **Scaler**

Something to Do
Look in the school or public library for books about the dentist and his work. Here are two books you may like:
Let's Go to a Dentist *by Naomi Buchheimer (Putnam).*
Dentists' Tools *by Carolyn Lapp (Lerner).*

Why Are Different-Shaped Teeth Useful?

If you have examined a model of the teeth, or if you have noticed some of your teeth after they have come out, you know that the teeth have different shapes. Having different-shaped teeth in the mouth helps you chew food better.

Teeth of different shapes do different jobs, although they all work together to chew or break up the food you eat.

The teeth in your upper jaw have the same general shapes as the corresponding teeth in your lower jaw. Dentists, by the way, use the word *maxillary* when referring to the upper jaw and *mandible* for the lower jaw.

The front teeth in your mouth are called *incisors*. There are eight of these incisors, four in the upper jaw and four in the lower jaw. The incisors have straight, sharp edges, and they cut the food much as a pair of scissors would do. For example, when you eat an apple or a stalk of celery, it is the incisors that are first used to bite off the pieces.

Then you move the pieces of food to the sides of your mouth. Here the *cuspids,* the teeth next to the incisors, tear the pieces into still smaller bits. A cuspid gets its name from the fact that its grinding surface has one *cusp* or point.

You have four cuspids in your mouth—one on the right and left side above and one on the right and left side below. The sharp points of your cuspids are needed to tear apart such foods as coarse fruits, vegetables, and meat.

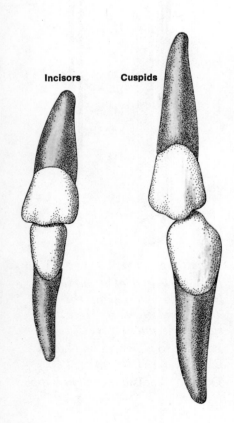

Incisors　　**Cuspids**

90

Next to the cuspids in your first set of teeth are the *primary molars*. But sometime between the ages of nine and eleven, you lose your primary molars. Teeth called *bicuspids* grow in to replace them. The bicuspids have two points or cusps. You will have eight of these bicuspids—two on each side of your upper and lower jaws.

After the cuspids have torn the food apart, your tongue moves the ball of food still farther back. Here the upper and lower bicuspids come together like a nutcracker to break and crush the food into even smaller pieces.

When the bicuspids have finished their work, you really begin to chew the food. You do this chewing with the *molars,* which are in the back part of the mouth. Your molars have broad tops with four or five cusps on them. The molars grind the food into very tiny bits.

When all your second or permanent teeth have come in, you will have twelve molars—three on each side of the upper jaw and three on each side of the lower jaw. The last molars will probably not come in until after your seventeenth birthday.

The first permanent molars come in when a child is about six years old. Because of the child's age when they come in, these teeth are known as *six-year molars.* These six-year molars are often called the most important teeth in the mouth. They must do the heavy work of chewing while the primary teeth are being replaced by the other permanent teeth. They also guide the other permanent molars, as they come in, into proper position.

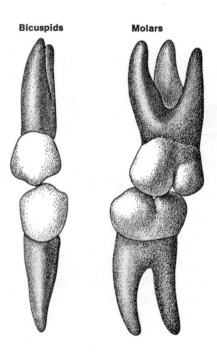

Bicuspids   **Molars**

Why Do You Need Your Teeth?

Every tooth has its special work to do, and every tooth is needed in the mouth.

The teeth in your upper and lower jaws work together to cut and tear and grind your food. If even a few teeth are missing, there will be empty spaces in your mouth. Then your teeth cannot work together so well to do their most important job, which is to start the digestion of food by chewing it properly.

There are some other reasons, though, why you need your teeth. You need them to help you speak clearly. You need your teeth especially to help you pronounce correctly words that have letters such as *f, g, j,* and *s* in them. Try saying *fifty, gum, jelly,* and *scissors.* Notice what your teeth do as you say these words. So you see that your teeth are important in your ability to communicate with others.

You need your teeth, too, to help give your face its proper shape. If too many permanent teeth are lost, the lower part of the face may change shape.

No other teeth will grow in to take the place of your permanent teeth. So you should take good care of every one of them. When the permanent teeth are lost, they can be replaced only by false teeth— which are expensive and usually less efficient than natural teeth.

Of course, teeth also help make a person look attractive. A pleasant, happy smile improves anyone's appearance; and when it shows clean, well-cared-for teeth, an impression is given of good general health.

Do You Know?
The teeth of a person who is a heavy smoker may not be attractive. Do you know why? Smoking can cause tobacco stains on the teeth.

92

Here you can see a complete set of the 32 permanent teeth. Which of these teeth are in your mouth now? Which teeth have yet to erupt, or come through?

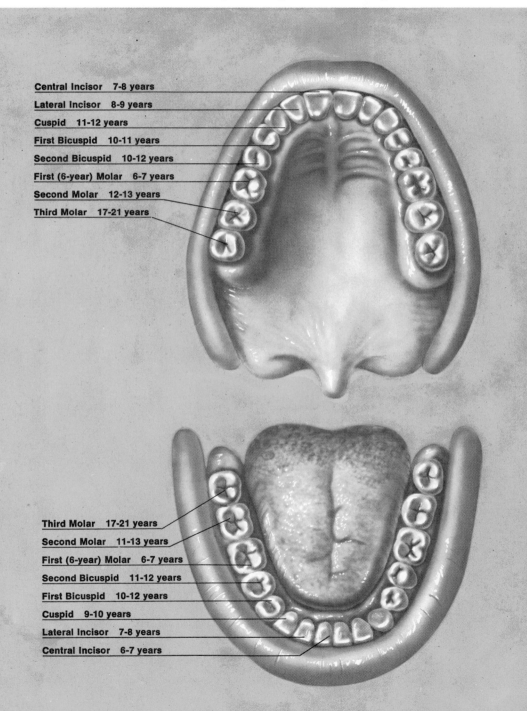

Central Incisor   7-8 years
Lateral Incisor   8-9 years
Cuspid   11-12 years
First Bicuspid   10-11 years
Second Bicuspid   10-12 years
First (6-year) Molar   6-7 years
Second Molar   12-13 years
Third Molar   17-21 years

Third Molar   17-21 years
Second Molar   11-13 years
First (6-year) Molar   6-7 years
Second Bicuspid   11-12 years
First Bicuspid   10-12 years
Cuspid   9-10 years
Lateral Incisor   7-8 years
Central Incisor   6-7 years

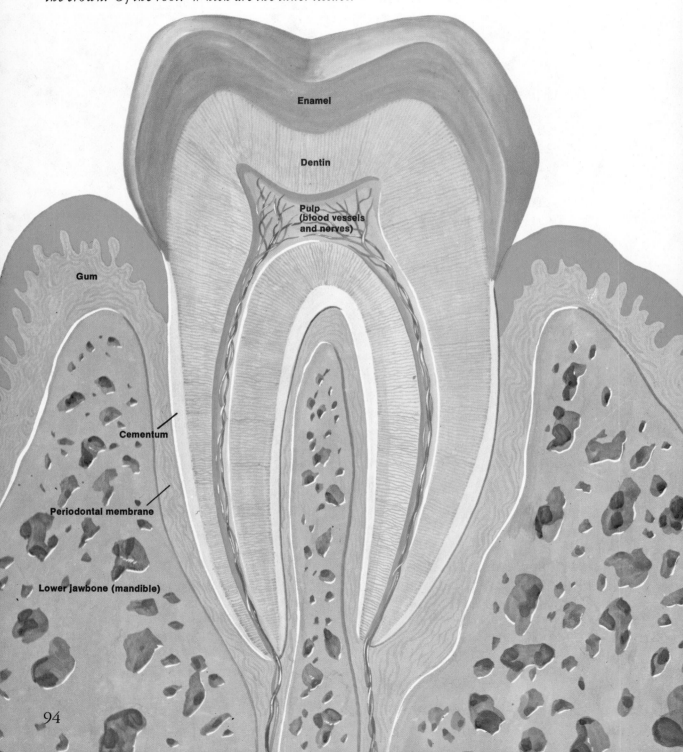

Here you can see the different parts of a tooth. What are the names of these parts? What is the outer covering of the crown? Of the root? Which are the inner tissues?

Enamel

Dentin

Pulp
(blood vessels
and nerves)

Gum

Cementum

Periodontal membrane

Lower jawbone (mandible)

Bacteria work on bits of foods, especially sweet, sticky foods left on the teeth. This causes acids to form which can break down the enamel.

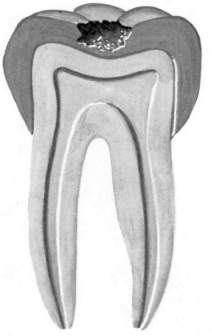

After the enamel is broken down, decay proceeds more rapidly in the dentin, causing a hole, or cavity. The patient may then have a toothache.

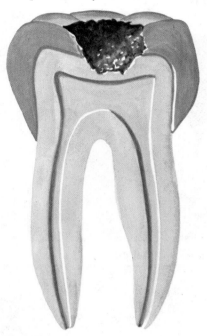

The cavity, if not filled, spreads into the pulp. This may cause pus or an abscess. Then the tooth may have to be extracted, or pulled.

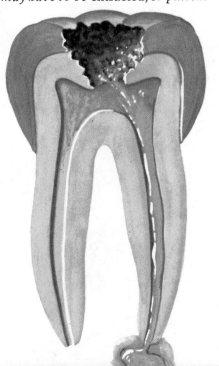

When the dentist finds a cavity, he cleans out the decay and then puts in a filling of silver or other material.

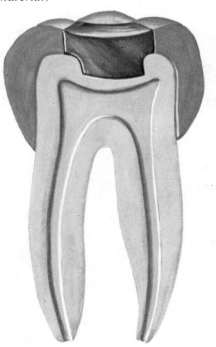

In this picture story of a boy's visit to the dentist, a tooth cavity is found and filled. Follow the story on these two pages.

1. Dentist's helper greets visitor.

2. Dentist fastens bib.

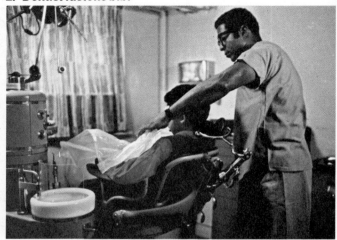

3. Dentist adjusts light.

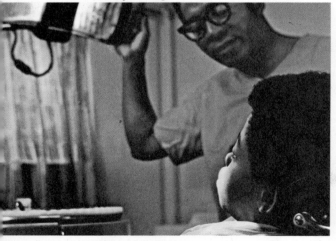

4. Dentist examines teeth.

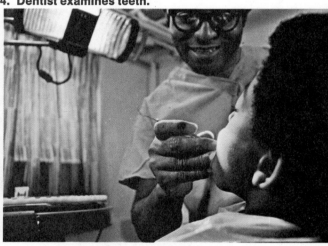

5. A cavity shows up in the mirror.

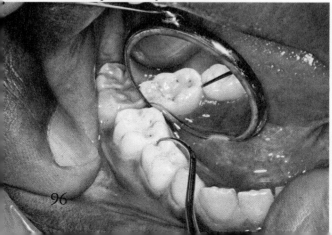

6. Dentist prepares cavity for filling.

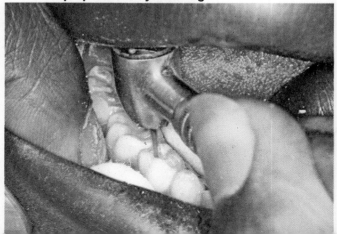

7. Mixed filling material is picked up.

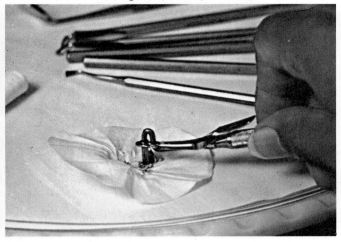

8. Filling is put in tooth.

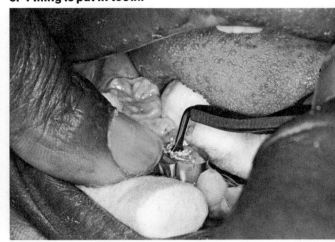

9. Excess filling material is scraped off.

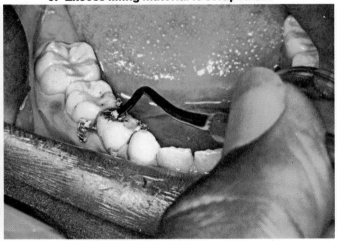

10. Bite is tested with new filling in place.

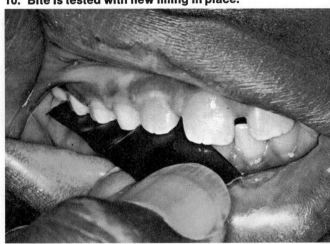

11. Filling material is given a final polishing.

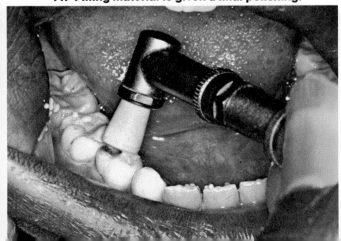

12. "Good bye. We'll see you soon."

97

You can see here some pictures of decay in different kinds of teeth. All pictures are enlarged cross-section views.

Bicuspid: The start of decay

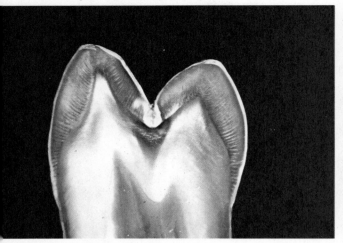

Bicuspid: A small cavity

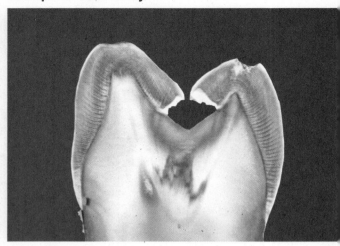

Molar: Large cavity

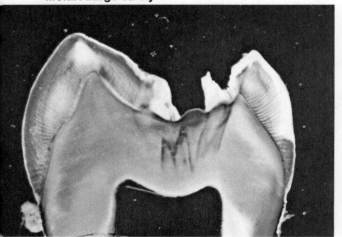

Molar: Decay into dentin

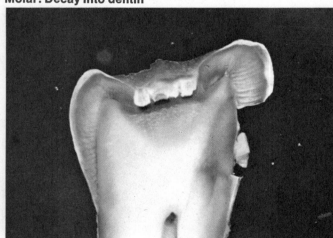

Incisor: Decay into pulp

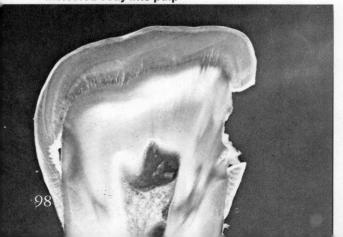

Molar: Much decay into the pulp

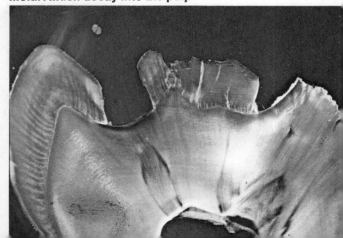

Health Questions Boys and Girls Often Ask

What Research Is Being Done on Tooth Care?

Dental research is going on all the time. The purpose of the research is to find better ways to take care of the teeth and to prevent tooth decay.

For example, there is dental research on the problem of reducing decay by the use of *fluorides.* Scientists are asking whether there are better chemicals than fluoride to use in painting the teeth. And they are trying out the chemicals called *phosphates.* It has already been discovered that phosphates prevent tooth decay in animals. Later research may prove that phosphates may prevent cavities in humans too.

Other research scientists have been testing a plastic colorless liquid. The dentist covers the teeth with this liquid. As the plastic dries, it forms a seal over the surfaces of the teeth. To keep the teeth protected, the plastic is put on about every six months.

In recent years it has been discovered that sometimes a tooth which has been accidentally knocked out can be replanted in the jaw by a dentist. Moreover, researchers are learning to make artificial teeth that can be put in the jaw's natural tooth sockets. Research of this kind has been conducted so far with baboons. It is hoped, though, that in the future when a human tooth has been knocked out, an artificial one can be used.

A new instrument that has been developed is called a *fluorometer.* You can see it at the right.

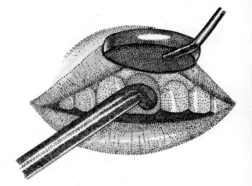

The dentist uses the fluorometer, *shown here, to detect cavities at the very earliest stage.*

99

The fluorometer can bathe the teeth in ultraviolet light. Ultraviolet light is light that you cannot see with your eyes; but when teeth are placed in the path of this invisible light, they glow, or *fluoresce*. The glow changes in places where cavities are about to start.

How Would an Astronaut Take Care of a Toothache?

Did you ever wonder what an astronaut would do if he had a toothache while he was on a space flight? This problem *has* been thought about by the Air Force research dentists. As you can imagine, the complicated equipment on a space ship takes the full attention of the crew. If a member of the crew had a severe toothache, problems could come up that might cause the failure of a space flight.

Air Force dentists have been working to solve the problems that might be caused by such tooth troubles. They have made a do-it-yourself dental kit that will be used by astronauts on the long trips expected in the future. The kit weighs 1 1/2 pounds and contains 26 items to help the space crew deal with toothache and dental emergencies.

Astronauts also have a problem with brushing the teeth. In simulated flights it has been found that ordinary toothpaste does not work. Detergent in the toothpaste causes foam to form in one of the water systems of the space capsule. Also, the oils in the toothpaste fill the space cabin with odors that can become sickening. Therefore, a method has been worked out for spacemen on short trips to use a dry toothbrush. In addition, they use dental floss to remove bits of food from between the teeth. For

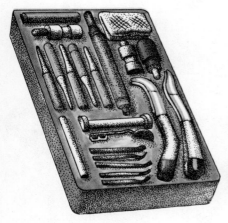

A Do-It-Yourself Kit for astronauts is shown here.

the longer space flights of the future, a tasteless, odorless toothpaste has been developed that can be swallowed by the user.

How Does Brushing Help the Teeth?

To answer this question, you need to know about *plaque.* Plaque is a sticky, colorless film of harmful bacteria which is always forming on the teeth. Even in a healthy mouth, plaque will be found. Plaque, if not removed daily, can build up along the gum line and injure the gums.

Certain bacteria in the plaque change sticky, sweet foods into acids. These acids begin the process of tooth decay.

Within minutes after you eat, the bacteria in your mouth start working on bits of sweet food to produce acid. That is why you should brush your teeth right after eating whenever it is possible to do so.

Brushing your teeth also makes them look better and feel cleaner. On the next page are some pictures that show you how to brush your teeth. What are the different things you should do?

The kind of toothbrush you use in cleaning your teeth is important, too. It should have a *flat* brushing surface and *soft* bristles. It should also be small enough to reach all parts of your mouth. Today, many families use electric toothbrushes. Some of these can do a good cleaning job if used according to directions. Your dentist can advise you about electric toothbrushes.

If you wonder about what kind of toothpaste to use, you might ask your dentist for help. Or

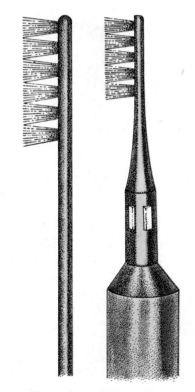

A good toothbrush has a flat brushing surface and soft bristles.

use a fluoride toothpaste that has on its container a statement by the American Dental Association (ADA).

How Else Can You Care for the Teeth?

There are some other things you can do to protect your teeth besides brushing them after you eat. Be careful not to crack the enamel on them. When the enamel on the teeth is cracked, cavities are likely to form. To keep the enamel free from cracks, you should avoid using your teeth to bite anything hard such as nuts or hard candy or ice.

You can also try to get enough of the right kinds of food each day, and try to limit the amount of sweets you eat, especially the sticky sweets that cling to your teeth. These encourage the mouth bacteria which cause tooth decay. When you do eat sweets, preferably at the end of a meal, be sure to follow with tooth brushing and flossing if at all possible.

Regular visits to your dentist are important, too, so that he or she can help protect your teeth. The dentist can also show you good ways to brush and floss your teeth. (One way to brush your teeth is shown in the drawings at the left.)

Some communities today add small amounts of fluorides to the drinking water if fluorides are not already present in the water. This is known as *fluoridation*. Children who drink fluoridated water tend to develop a hard tooth enamel that helps prevent tooth decay.

If you live in a community where there is not enough fluoride in the drinking water, your den-

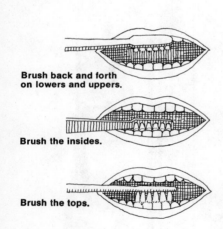

Brush back and forth on lowers and uppers.

Brush the insides.

Brush the tops.

For front teeth, upper and lower, also make up and down strokes with front of brush over the teeth and gum tissue.

Besides brushing the teeth, you should also use dental floss to remove the plaque between your teeth.

102

tist may "paint" your teeth from time to time with a fluoride solution. This painting of the teeth by the dentist gives considerable protection against tooth decay.

Why Are Permanent Teeth Sometimes Out of Place?

To understand why permanent teeth do not always grow in their proper position, you need to think about how and when the first and second sets of teeth come in.

Most children get all their first set of teeth, or *primary* teeth, by the time they are two and a half or three years old. Some of these teeth begin to get loose and come out by the age of six or seven or thereabouts, but not all of them are lost until a child is eleven or twelve years of age.

The second set of teeth, or *permanent* teeth, form under the primary teeth, as you see in the picture at the right. When a primary tooth comes out too soon, the tooth or teeth next to it may grow over and fill part of the space that is left. Then there will not be enough room for the new teeth to grow in their proper positions.

Something can be done, though, if a primary tooth is lost too soon. The dentist may suggest replacing the lost tooth with a *space maintainer,* which will hold the space until a permanent tooth comes in. The space maintainer will also keep the other teeth in their proper position so that chewing is not interfered with. Or the dentist may advise you to see an *orthodontist.* An orthodontist is a dentist who has had special training in handling problems of irregular teeth.

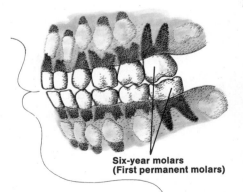

**Six-year molars
(First permanent molars)**

The roots of the primary teeth are dissolving while the permanent teeth are forming under the gums in the jawbone.

103

Check Yourself

1. Look back at the questions on page 88. How would you answer them now?

2. How would you explain each of these terms?

    a. cementum

    b. dentin

    c. enamel

    d. orthodontist

    e. periodontal membrane

    f. pulp

3. How do these kinds of teeth help you in chewing food?

    a. cuspids

    b. incisors

    c. molars

4. What are two good reasons for brushing the teeth?

5. What is fluoridation?

6. Why are teeth sometimes out of place in the jaw?

7. What are three important jobs teeth do for us?

8. What kinds of research are being done on the care of the teeth?

Things to Do

1. Plan and be ready to give a talk that would be suitable for first- or second-graders on care of the teeth.

2. Choose a volunteer to write to the American Dental Association, 211 East Chicago Avenue, Chicago, Illinois 60611. The writer can ask for single copies of any free materials on dental health.

3. Make posters on the work of the dentist, including some of the dentist's helpers. Refer to the pictured material on pages 96 and 97.

4. Look in newspapers or magazines for material about teeth or about new equipment to aid in detecting cavities. Bring the clippings to school for display.

5. The class might develop a filmstrip about the teeth, suggesting pictures that could be included.

6. Through the local dental society, a dentist might be located and invited to talk to your class.

7. If your dentist has shown you how to floss your teeth with dental floss, describe the correct procedure to your class.

Use a ruler or a strip of paper to cover the answer column at the right. Read the first item and write the missing word or words on a piece of paper. Then move your ruler or paper strip down to uncover the answer and see if you are right. Go on in the same way with each of the other items. Do not write in this book.

The numbers by the answers show the pages in this book that give information about the subject. For the items you miss, go back and review this information.

1. The three main parts of the tooth are the ———, ———, and ———.

crown, neck, roots 88

2. A tooth is made of four kinds of tissue: ———, ———, ———, and ———.

enamel, dentin, cementum, pulp 88

3. The white covering of the crown of the tooth is called ———.

enamel 88

4. When decay spreads into the ——— of your tooth, you are likely to have a toothache.

dentin 89

5. Another name for *dental caries* is tooth ———.

decay 89

6. Mouth ——— work on sweet foods left in the mouth and cause decay.

bacteria 95

7. The best kind of toothbrush is one with a ——— brushing surface.

flat 101

8. The best time to brush the teeth is right ——— you eat.

after 101

9. A community's water supply can be ——— to protect the teeth of people living in the community.

fluoridated 102

Health Test for Unit Four

Copy each number on a piece of paper. After the number write the correct answer, *true* or *false*.

1. The enamel on teeth is very soft.

2. If the enamel on a tooth is injured, new enamel will be formed.

3. A dentist removes tartar with an instrument called a scaler.

4. All teeth have four roots.

5. Tooth decay always begins on the outside of a tooth.

6. The chewing surface of a cuspid has one point.

7. The chewing surface of a bicuspid has two points.

8. Molars cut and tear the food you eat.

9. Another name for first teeth is primary teeth.

10. All the permanent teeth have come in by the time a boy or girl is eight years old.

11. One reason why you need your teeth is to help you speak clearly.

12. The cementum covers the root of the tooth.

13. Dental caries is another name used for dentin.

14. Tartar is good for the gums.

15. Six-year molars are permanent teeth.

16. Bacteria in the mouth help cause tooth decay.

17. A good way to help avoid tooth cavities is to cut down on the sweet food and soft drinks in your diet.

18. Little or no dental health research is now being carried on.

19. The dental hygienist is a helper who cleans the teeth.

20. There are blood vessels and nerves in the pulp.

21. A tooth that has been knocked out can sometimes be replanted in the mouth.

22. An orthodontist does very little besides clean teeth.

23. Cracking nuts can help strengthen the enamel on the teeth.

24. The inside surfaces of the teeth should be brushed too.

25. Your toothbrush should have a flat brushing surface and soft bristles.

Number of Answers   25

Number Right   _____

Score (Number Right × 4)   _____

5 How Will You Play?

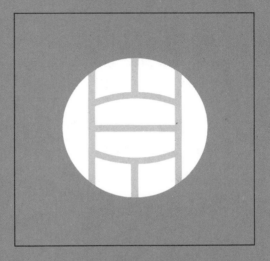

There is lots of activity in this unit. You will learn how to play some active games, and you will explore some of the many different ways your body can move. There are stunts to try, too. And you will have a chance to think about what it means to be a good sport.

1. What are some of the advantages of active games and sports?

2. How do you play Guard the Castle? Keep Away? Bounce-Ball Relay?

3. What is the value in exploring movements such as different ways to run or hop or jump?

4. In what ways do we show how we feel?

5. How can good posture help you?

What Do You Like to Play?

Maybe you know how to play the game Tug of War. Read the poem "Tug of War" on the facing page and see if it gives you some ideas about how to play the game. See the picture opposite and the photograph of the game on page 113.

What is another game that is fun to play? Why do you enjoy it?

Active games are not only fun to play; they also help you stretch your muscles and give you a change of pace from quiet activities such as studying or watching television. Active games have other benefits, too. What are some of these benefits?

On pages 110 to 116 you can learn more about some games that boys and girls your age usually like. Study the directions and pictures for each game until you know how to play it. As soon as you can, try to play the game on the playground.

Tug of War

No one is quite sure
how to win at Tug of War
except that you pull
and pullll and pulllllll
and just as you're sure
you are winning,
the other team pulls
and pulllls and pullllllls
and you fall their way
and then they fall your way
but
if everyone on your team
should suddenly take a big breath
and tug all together
with arms around each other
then you might just possibly win.

Can You Play Guard the Castle?

How would you explain to someone how to play Guard the Castle? Read the directions below to check your explanation.

Players: Nine to twelve
Place: Gym or playground
Equipment: Basketball, three empty milk cartons

Draw two circles, a large one for the players, and a smaller one for the three empty cartons.

All players except one, who is the guard, stand on the big circle. The guard stands near the little circle which has the empty milk cartons inside it.

Players on the big circle try to knock over one or more of the empty cartons by throwing the ball at them. The guard tries to keep the players from doing this. He may stop the ball with his hands, feet, or body.

A player who knocks over a carton with the ball—or makes the guard do it while he is trying to guard the cartons—takes over as the new guard. The old guard then goes to the outer circle as a player.

Sometimes it is a good idea for a player *not* to try and throw the ball at the carton. It may be better for him to quickly pass the ball to a team-mate across the circle and catch the guard with his back to the ball.

Now look at the photograph of boys and girls playing this game on page 114. How would you answer the questions asked there?

Guard the Castle

110

How Do You Play Keep Away?

Read the directions below for Keep Away, then be ready to tell how to play this game.

Players: Two teams with three to six players on each team
Place: Large circle, fifteen to twenty feet across
Equipment: One soccer ball, basketball, or rubber playground ball; colored ties around wrist or arm, one color for each team.

Draw a large circle with chalk. Keep the circle well away from walls or equipment.

The team with the ball stands just outside the large circle. Players on the opposing team are inside the circle. The players inside try to get the ball as the opposing team passes the ball back and forth across the circle.

If the team inside the circle catches the ball—or if the ball is dropped by a member of the opposite team—the team inside the circle changes places with the team outside.

You can speed up the game by allowing the player with the ball only five seconds to throw it. If he fails to get rid of the ball in that time, it is turned over to the other team.

You can make the game more difficult by requiring players to bounce the ball to their teammates rather than throw it.

Now look at the photograph of the boys playing Keep Away on page 115. How would you answer the questions above the picture?

Keep Away

How Do You Play Bounce-Ball Relay?

After you have read the directions below for Bounce-Ball Relay, be ready to tell others how to play the game.

Players: Two or more teams made up of three or four players each
Place: Gym or playground
Equipment: Rubber ball or basketball for each team

Each team lines up single file behind a starting line. Have a five-foot space between each team.

Draw a goal line about 25 or 35 feet in front of the starting line.

At a signal, the first person on each team bounces a ball with one hand up to the goal line; he or she then runs back fast, carrying the ball.

The ball is handed to the person on the team who is now at the head of the line, and the first runner goes to the back of the team's line.

The player who received the ball now bounces it with one hand to the goal line. He or she runs back with the ball and gives it to the player at the head of the line on his or her team.

The game continues in this way until everyone on the team has a turn.

The first team to have all its players bounce the ball to the goal line and return to the starting line wins.

Now look at the photograph of young people actually playing this game on page 116. How would you answer the questions above the picture?

Bounce-Ball Relay

When does one team win this game from the other? Can you explain how to play this game? Why is a game like Tug of War good for you?

114

115

What game is being played here? How could you change
this game into another relay game? What are some safety
ideas to keep in mind when you play relays?

Can You Move in These Ways?

You can become more skillful in games and sports if you take time to explore and practice some of the movements used in these games and sports. Here are some problem-solving movements you may want to explore.

1. Can you run and stop quickly when you hear a signal such as a whistle?

2. Can you combine a run with another movement such as a jump?

3. Can you run backwards? Sideways? Can you zigzag as you run?

4. As you run forward, can you change from stretching tall to making yourself very small?

5. How many ways can you move while two feet stay in place? While one foot stays in place?

6. How far can you stretch out as you stand in your own space?

7. Can you write a number in the air with your arm? Can you make the same number on the floor by running?

8. In how many *different* ways can you move across the room?

9. Can you run about with others in a given space without any collisions?

10. Can you show, with a real or imaginary ball, how many different things you can do with it?

11. Can you combine a hop with another movement such as a skip, a jump, or a run?

12. Can you go around in a circle by jumping? In a square? In a triangle?

Can you move like the boy in these pictures?

Can Body Movement Show How You Feel?

You may not have thought about it, but you often do show how you feel by the way you move about.

Think how you would use body movements to show the following things.

1. How might you move about if you were feeling *sad?*

2. How might you move about if you were feeling *angry?*

3. How might you move about if you were feeling *shy* or *left out of things?*

4. Act out each of these words:

fright   impatience   curiosity
excitement   bossiness   worry

5. Suppose you have been helping clean house all day and you are *tired.* How might you show that you are tired by the way you move about?

6. Act out each of the words below with body movements. A volunteer might choose one of these words to act out; then the watchers can try to guess the word.

busy   silly   puzzled
lazy   nervous   peppy

7. How might you move about if you were feeling very *proud?*

8. How might you move about if you were feeling *disappointed* about something?

9. Choose any word you want that describes how people sometimes feel. Be ready to act out the word. The others in your class will try to guess what the word is.

What feelings are being acted out in these pictures?

118

What Can You Do About Posture?

As you know, it helps to think about good posture when you are sitting or standing, working or playing. Good posture not only makes you look better, but it can help you move about and do things without getting tired too soon.

When you are standing up to iron, cook, or wash dishes, it is a good idea to stand erect with the weight on both feet. Poor posture makes tasks harder and more tiring than they need to be.

When you are doing jobs like mopping or sweeping, to avoid strain, keep your back straight and your weight balanced on both feet.

When you are trying to lift things, use your strong leg muscles instead of your back muscles to make your work easier. Your leg muscles are longer and stronger than your back muscles.

Another thing to remember is to wear shoes that fit you. It is not easy to have good posture when your shoes hurt your feet—and when you walk as if every step hurt you! Shoes that fit well are ones that are long enough and wide enough for your feet. Shoes should be about one-half inch longer than your feet.

The most important thing you can do to improve your posture is, of course, to try to keep strong and well. Good posture is often a sign that a person is strong and healthy and is following good health practices, including managing upset feelings in a wholesome way. In other words, good posture usually goes along with good total health.

Use your strong leg muscles instead of your back muscles when lifting something heavy.

Things to Do

1. Unscramble the words in the list of items below and you will have a code for good sports. Check your answer with Item 4 on page 121. Can you add to the list of items in this code?

a. A doog trops syalp riaf dna seirt ot niw, oot.

b. A doog trops sekat snrut.

c. A doog trops si a doog resol.

d. A doog trops syebo eht selur.

e. A doog trops sniw tuohtiw gniggarb.

f. A doog trops seod ton truh rehto s'elpoep sgnileef.

2. Think of a time when you have seen someone being a good sport. Then write about what you saw.

3. Besides games and sports, another way to relax and have fun is to have a hobby. Some children collect things, some like to draw or paint, others like to put together models, and still others like to cook. Be ready to tell what *your* hobby is.

Maybe your class will want to have a hobby show.

4. When you are out on the playground, you may want to try the stunt called Pull Over. It takes two people to do this stunt.

First draw a line. You stand on one side of the line, and the other person stands on the other side.

You put your right hand in the right hand of the other player. At a signal, you try to pull the other person over the line. And he tries to pull you over the line.

5. You may also want to try some other stunts you know. Be able to explain and demonstrate two or three stunts to the class.

6. You may want to look up your favorite sport in an encyclopedia. For example, if you look up *baseball,* you may learn how the game got started, how a baseball is made, and many other interesting things. Later you can tell others some of the things you have learned.

More Things to Do

1. Did you know that children for hundreds of years have been enjoying some of the same games and stunts? Look for this book at the library. It tells about a famous painting called "Children's Games." The painting shows games that were played by Flemish children over four hundred years ago. The picture  was painted by Peter Breughel the Elder, a Flemish artist.

Find out what some of the games and stunts were that have been favorites over the years since Breughel painted the picture "Children's Games."

2. Draw a picture of *your* favorite game or sport and be ready to tell or write about why you enjoyed it.

3. Listen as your teacher reads the poem in the next column to your class. Try to "see" a picture of the runner.

Later you may want to make a picture of the runner that this poem tells about.

The Runner

By Walt Whitman

On a flat road runs the well-trained runner,
He is lean and sinewy with muscular legs,
He is thinly clothed, he leans forward as he
runs,
With lightly closed fists and arms partially
raised.

4. The answer to the good sports' code is as follows:

a. A good sport plays fair and tries to win, too.
b. A good sport takes turns.
c. A good sport is a good loser.
d. A good sport obeys the rules.
e. A good sport wins without bragging.
f. A good sport does not hurt other people's feelings.

Check Yourself

1. Look back at the questions on page 108. How would you answer them now?

2. What are some safety problems in relays and how can they be avoided?

3. How should you pick up a heavy package from the ground? Be ready to demonstrate how to do it.

4. What is a nontiring posture for a person to use who is standing at the sink to wash dishes? Be ready to demonstrate this posture.

5. What posture helps keep you from getting tired when you are mopping a floor? Be ready to demonstrate this posture.

6. In which of these three games—Bounce-Ball Relay, Keep Away, and Guard the Castle—do you throw and catch a ball?

In which of these games must you be able to dribble a ball?

Special Research

1. Look up your favorite sport in the encyclopedia. For example, if you look up *baseball,* you may learn how the game got started, how a baseball is made, and many other interesting things.

Later you can tell your class some of the things you have learned.

2. Look in the school or public library for books about sports and how to play them. Some books you may like are these:

The First Book of Baseball by Benjamin Brewster (Watts).

The First Book of Swimming by Donald Schiffer (Watts).

3. You might want to look in the library for some sports stories such as these:

Baseball Flyhawk by Matt Christopher (Little, Brown).

Bats and Balls by Beman Lord (Walck).

Mystery Guest at Left End by Beman Lord (Walck).

The Year Mom Won the Pennant by Matt Christopher (Little, Brown).

Watch Those Red Wheels Roll by Marion Renick (Scribner).

6 How Safety-Minded Are You?

Do you have the safety knowledge you need to look ahead and prevent accidents? This unit will give information that can help you avoid the kinds of accidents most likely to happen to boys and girls your age. The unit will also help you review some safety and first-aid practices.

Read to Find Out

1. What are some safety guides to use when you walk along a road that has no sidewalk?

2. What are some safety ideas you should keep in mind when climbing? When throwing? When flying a kite?

3. What are some safety guides for softball players? For swimmers? For boaters?

4. What are some gun-safety rules?

5. What are some safety precautions to follow when you use electric equipment?

6. How could you help someone who is having difficulty in the water? How might you help yourself?

Why Do You Need to Be Safety-Minded?

Every day you make safety decisions. You have to decide whether an action is safe or whether you or others may be hurt by what you plan to do.

For example, even in such a simple, everyday thing as going down some stairs, you have safety decisions to make. What are some of them?

In doing such ordinary things as walking, climbing, and throwing, accidents can happen. And, at your age, accidents are quite likely to occur in play activities, in home and school situations, around water, and with firearms.

That is why you need to become safety-minded —to learn and use safe ways of doing things.

What Do You Think?
What do you think this safety slogan means: Safety Starts Between the Ears?
What parts of the body help keep you safe?

124

How Can You Keep Safe When Walking?

Can you think of some safety precautions a pedestrian should use when walking where there is no sidewalk—as the boys are doing in the picture below? What are some precautions for walking at dusk?

Now turn to page 126. Compare your answers with the safety ideas given there. Be ready to explain the reason behind each safety idea.

Also look for safety guides to follow when you are walking in a group, crossing an intersection, carrying an umbrella.

When you have to walk where there is no sidewalk, you should be careful to walk where you can see the oncoming cars. *This means that you should keep to the left of the street or road.*

It is a good idea, too, to walk single file on a road that has no sidewalks. And, if you are walking at dusk or at night, be sure to wear something light or white—or carry a light.

When you are walking in a group, you must remember to be as careful as you are when you are walking alone. This means that you will be on the alert for traffic and traffic signs—and that you will not "just follow along" with the group and fail to observe your usual caution.

If there are crosswalks at an intersection, be sure to use them. They are for your protection. Motorists expect you in crosswalks, and it is only there that you have the right of way. However, even in a crosswalk, keep alert. Cross only at corners or in crosswalks. Don't be a jaywalker.

Keep in mind, too, that not all intersections are equally safe for pedestrians to cross. Some have crosswalks and some do not. Some intersections have traffic lights or policemen or traffic guards to aid you and some do not. Therefore, in planning a walking route try to map a way for yourself that uses the intersections with the most safety aids.

At a crossing, look both ways before you start to cross the street; and always look behind you for turning cars, too.

Wait on the curb—not on the street—for turning cars to pass.

Something to Do
See how many good safety guides you can suggest for this topic:
How Can You Keep Safe When Running?

126

How Can You Keep Safe When Climbing?

Suppose you have moved to a new neighborhood and that you have found a tree you want to climb—like the boy in the picture below. What safety ideas should be kept in mind?

What safety guides should you follow if you are climbing hills?

Do you think it is safe to climb on fences? Why or why not?

Now turn to page 128 to learn some safety guides when climbing. Think of reasons for these guides.

When you are climbing a *tree,* you want to be sure to choose one that has low branches and rough bark. Do not climb too high in a tree, since height increases the danger of broken bones if you should fall. If the bark of a tree is rough, this can help keep you from slipping as you climb.

Some trees have dead branches on them, and you will want to stay off those. Such branches can be dangerous to climbers. Why?

Sometimes a tree has electric wires passing through it. Be sure to avoid a tree like this when you are looking for one to climb. Why?

Often when you are on a hike or a camping trip, you will find a *hill* you would like to climb. This can be fun, but you will want to walk and not run when you come down the hill. Why?

Some cliffs have overhanging places, or ledges. There may be fences or guard rails to keep you from getting too close to the edge of such cliffs. But if you are not protected by such aids, stay away from the ledges. What is the reason for this warning?

Most *fences* are dangerous to climb on, too. Stay off spiked fences and barbed-wire ones. In fact you should not climb any fence without permission.

Other places that are not safe to climb on are *roofs* and *partly constructed new buildings.* There is always the danger of falling from such places.

On the other hand, your playground may have *climbing ladders* and other *climbing equipment.* If so, remember to take turns and to stay off the equipment when it is wet. Why?

Something to Talk Over
Do you ever do any climbing on ladders? *If so, what are some safety practices you should keep in mind?*

128

What About Safety When Throwing?

Suppose you have been asked to make a report to the class on "Safety When Throwing," and you want to arrange an exhibit on the subject—as the girl in the picture below is doing. You want to show objects that are *safe* to throw and objects that are *not safe* to throw. What objects would you put with the group of things that are safe to throw? What objects would you put with the group of things that are not safe to throw?

Be ready to explain the choices you made. Then compare your ideas with those on the next page.

Things that are safe to throw.

Things that are not safe to throw.

The first thing to keep in mind about safety when throwing is to throw only those things that are supposed to be thrown—things like softballs, rubber-tipped darts, footballs, bean bags, model airplanes, toy gliders.

If this practice is followed, no one will get hurt by flying rocks or pointed objects. And no one will have to see a doctor because sand or dirt has been thrown in his eyes or ears.

Some things, however, like ropes and snowballs are sometimes safe to throw and sometimes not safe. For example, it is fun to throw a rope, and it is all right to throw it around a post or something like that. But you should not throw a rope around a person. If you do that, you might make him have a bad fall. Or the rope might choke him and stop his breathing.

Snowballs, too, are fun to throw if you avoid injury with them. If you want to throw snowballs, it is safer to throw them at a target. Be sure that no one is in the way who might get hit.

Be sure, too, that you do not throw a snowball that could strike the windshield of a car. What could happen to the driver if the windshield of his car were hit?

Even with things that are supposed to be thrown, such as softballs and rubber-tipped darts, you will want to be safety-minded. For instance, you will not throw a ball to someone unless you know he is expecting it. And you will always make sure that the darts have safety tips on them before you throw them at the target.

Something to Do
The school nurse might be invited to talk to the group about playground accidents that have been reported to her. A discussion should follow on how the various accidents could have been avoided.

130

How Do You Fly a Kite Safely?

Now suppose that you have just finished making a kite. All you need is some string to fly it with.

You look around the house and find two kinds of string to choose from—as the boy has in the picture below. One is a ball of ordinary string. And the other is a ball of Christmas string that has some tinsel or some metallic threads in it. Which ball of string is the safe one to use? To find out, turn the page.

Also find out about safe places and safe *weather* for kite flying.

Kite flying can be dangerous unless you have the right kind of string. A kite string should have no wire or tinsel or metal in it. The string should also be kept dry, which means you should never fly your kite in stormy weather.

Metallic kite string and wet string would be unsafe choices because electricity could be carried very easily along them.

Electricity from a stroke of lightning could flash right down a string with metal on it or a wet string. Unlike Benjamin Franklin who was lucky in his kite-flying experiment, many kite flyers *have* been killed by electric currents carried down a wet kite string! If you do not know the story of Benjamin Franklin and his famous experiment, you might look it up in the library. Two books you might look for are listed at the left.

For your kite flying, you should try to find a large, vacant area that is safe for such play. A playground, a vacant lot, or an open field might be good choices. When you find a place of this kind, be sure to check for any rocks or holes or other hazards that could cause you to trip or fall.

Be careful about flying kites in places that are near railroads and power lines. If ever a kite you are flying should tangle with a power line, the safe thing to do is leave the kite where it is. Do not make any efforts to get it down. High voltage wires can be extremely dangerous.

And, of course, you know that you should always avoid running in or across a street when you are flying a kite.

Something to Do
Two books on Benjamin Franklin that you might find are these:
Benjamin Franklin *by Ingri and Edgar P. d'Aulaire. (Doubleday).*
Ben Franklin of Old Philadelphia *by Margaret Cousins. (Random). Volunteers might prepare reports on these books.*

How Can You Keep Safe When Playing Softball?

Suppose you are playing softball and are at bat, like the girl in the picture below.

After you have hit a ball pitched to you, what will you do with the bat?

Now turn the page. Compare your answer with the safety guide about bats.

Also look for ideas to help you answer these questions:

What are some causes of accidents that happen in softball playing?

How can such accidents be prevented?

Following are some safety guides for softball players.

See if you can think of the reason or reasons behind each guide listed.

1. Drop—never throw—the bat after you have hit the ball. Never throw the bat, either, after you have struck out or after you have been walked to first base.

2. Play in a safe place; avoid playing in the street unless it is blocked off.

3. Check the play area for such things as stones, holes, broken glass.

4. Do not use stones or other hard objects for bases.

5. Wear safety equipment, such as face masks, when catching.

6. Do not *run* into the street or across it after the ball. Look both ways for cars and then *walk* into the street after the ball.

7. Catch high balls with fingers pointing upward and low balls with fingers pointing down toward the ground. Improper catching can result in hand and finger injuries.

8. Call the turn when catching pop flies; the first player to call has the right to catch it.

9. When you practice pitching and catching, be careful not to endanger pedestrians or little children who may be playing nearby.

10. Avoid sliding into bases, unless you have been taught how to slide safely.

What other softball safety ideas can you think of? Be ready to jot down your ideas for class use.

Something to Do
Prepare short lists of safety guides for using sleds *and* roller skates.

What Should You Do If You Find a Gun?

Suppose that you find a gun in an alley or some other place, like the girl in the picture below. What should you do about it?

Turn to page 136 to find the answer. Also find out the answers to these questions and be ready to give reasons for these answers:

What should you do if you find some bullets or shells?

What precautions should be taken if a gun is kept in a home?

Why should you *never* point a gun at anyone?

If you should ever find a gun outdoors, do not pick it up. And do not pick up bullets or shells that you may find. A loaded gun or shells or bullets that have been lying around outdoors sometimes become sensitive. If they are moved in any way, they may explode.

The safe thing to do is to tell your parents or some other adult about the gun or bullets or shells that you have found. An adult can report the location to the police or other responsible persons who are trained in the safe handling of firearms and ammunition.

If a gun is kept in your home, it should always be kept unloaded and stored out of the reach of children. Also, ammunition should be stored in a separate place. Many firearms accidents occur when children come upon a gun at home and start to play with it.

Never point a gun at anyone. Many people, thinking a gun was not loaded, have playfully pointed it at someone and pulled the trigger. All too often the gun was loaded and, as a result, a serious accident occurred.

Before a person of any age is allowed to use a gun, he should be taught how to use it by a trained instructor and on a well-protected range. Backyard target shooting is dangerous because a stray bullet might hit someone. Many communities have laws forbidding backyard target shooting within the city limits.

When you are older, if you ever plan to use a gun for a sport like skeet shooting, try to take a gun-safety course first.

Do You Know?
What is the safest color for a hunter to wear so he can be easily seen—and so he is not likely to be shot accidentally by another hunter?
Where else is this color now often used?

136

What Should You Do First?

Suppose you are in the kitchen washing dishes, like the girl in the picture below. Your sister calls to you and asks you to plug in the electric iron for her. What should you do *before* you plug in the iron? Why?

Compare your answer with the one on page 138. Also look for answers to such questions as these:

What is the safe way to put a cord into or take it out of a socket?

When is a cord not safe to use? What is the danger of running cords under a rug?

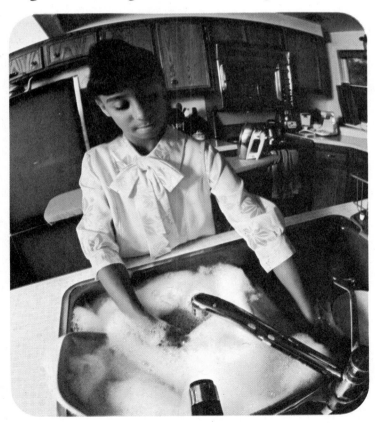

One important thing to remember is that when your body is wet it is easy for an electric current to come into the body through your skin. When this happens, you get an electric shock which can be painful and dangerous. *So never touch any electric equipment when you have wet hands—or when you are standing in a wet place.* You should make sure your hands are dry and that you are standing in a dry place when you plug in any electric equipment.

Remember, too, that cords for electric equipment have safety handles on them. *To avoid any chance of getting a shock, always use the safety handle when you plug a cord into—or take the cord out of—the electric socket.*

Sometimes when an electric cord gets old, the covering comes off the wires in places. You could get a shock by touching an old cord like this. Also a frayed cord can start a fire. *Do not touch a connected cord that has lost part of its covering. Such a cord should be thrown away or taken to an electric shop to be fixed.*

You may want to check around your house to see if there are any conditions with electric equipment that might cause dangerous situations. Here are some things to look for:

Electric cords running under rugs or held in place by nails. Such cords have more than the usual strain on them and are likely to become worn or frayed.

Too many lights or appliances connected into one wall socket by use of double sockets. Too much equipment plugged into an outlet can put a strain on the wiring and possibly lead to an electrical fire.

Do You Know?
What should you do if a piece of bread gets stuck in your electric toaster? Explain your answer.

What Could You Do to Help?

Suppose you are standing on a pier and you see a child fall off the pier into the water, like the boy in the picture. The child does not seem to know how to swim. How could you help?

Now read page 140 and see how your ideas compare with the ones given there.

Find out, too, how to help if someone falls overboard when you are boating.

What would you do if *you* should ever need to stay afloat in the water? Read page 141 to check your suggestions.

If you should see a person in trouble in the water, you should call loudly for help. If possible, send someone nearby to get help from an adult.

Meanwhile do not jump into the water to try to save the person. Even trained lifeguards have been pulled under water by struggling persons whom they were trying to save. By jumping in, you risk your own life and you may ruin any chance of saving the person you are trying to help.

If the person is near the shore or pier, lie down and try to grab his clothing and pull him to safety. Make sure you are anchored well enough to avoid being pulled in yourself.

If the person is farther out, find something you can extend to him, such as your belt or shirt, or an oar or fishing pole. Again be sure to anchor yourself firmly so he does not pull you in, too.

If the person is too far out for you to extend anything to him, throw something to keep him afloat. Use anything that floats, such as a life preserver, a beachball, an oar, a rubber tire, or a slab of wood.

If you are boating and someone falls overboard, throw him a life jacket, if he is not wearing one. If there are no life jackets, throw him anything that floats. Pull him to the side of the boat. Let him hang onto the side of the boat until he can pull himself into the boat. It is always a good practice when you go boating to wear a life jacket.

Never try to swim to shore if your boat overturns. Hang onto the boat until help arrives. Even expert swimmers have been overcome by exhaustion while trying to reach shore.

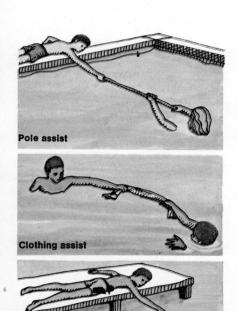

Pole assist

Clothing assist

Hand assist

If ever you should be in difficulty yourself in the water, there are things you can do to keep afloat until help comes.

The first thing to remember is to keep calm and avoid tiring yourself by thrashing around wildly.

Don't forget that it is easy to keep afloat. Your body has substances in it such as fat and air that help it float; and your lungs, when full of air, act as built-in life preservers.

Next, remember to use *survival floating*. This is how you do it:

1. Breathe, hold your breath, and then sink under water. Extend arms and legs downward as though standing in the water.

2. Let yourself float back to the surface. When your head is partly out, raise arms to sides. At the same time, stretch one leg forward and one back, as in the scissors kick.

3. To force head out of water, gently pull arms to sides and bring legs together. As arms come down, begin to exhale—until nose breaks surface. Inhale when mouth is out of water. Chin should not come out of water.

4. Take another breath and let yourself sink again. As you sink, give slight downward push with arms—it prevents you from sinking too deeply.

You can keep on following these steps in survival floating for a long time—for hours if necessary.

The next time you go swimming, practice survival floating while your parents or other adults in charge watch you.

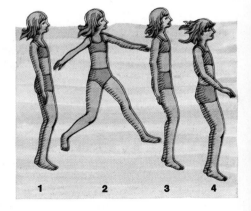

What are the four steps in survival floating?

141

What Are Unsafe Places to Play?

Did you know that there are some places that are especially unsafe and should always be *avoided* as places to play?

If you read a newspaper, you may at times have seen articles about young people who have been injured through careless play in dangerous places.

Can you think of any such places that are always unsafe for play?

Did you think of *wharves* or *pilings* or other waterfront places where there is danger of slipping and falling into deep water?

Or perhaps you thought of diggings, or *excavations,* where a cave-in of sand or soil could cause you to suffocate or to be crushed.

Playing on the roof of garages or of any other buildings is always hazardous, too. How would you explain why this is so?

If you live in a farm community, you may have thought of farm equipment, such as tractors. It is always unsafe to play on or around farm equipment. What are some reasons you might give for this safety precaution?

There are other unsafe places as well. Some of these places are shown in the pictures on pages 143 to 148. They include empty buildings, construction sites, railroad yards, city dumps, quarries, and parking lots.

Study these pictures carefully. Be ready to answer the questions that go with each of the pictures.

Something to Do
Can you unscramble these safety guides?
SATY WAYA RFMO ITCY UMPDS.
OD TON LPAY NI AILRODRA ARYDS.
EEPK WAAY MORF CONTSRUTOINC LPACSE.

142

You should not play in or around any kind of construction work. It is against the law to do so. What could cause accidents around construction work?

143

Parking lots with cars coming out of them can be dangerous play places. What are some accidents that might occur to those who choose such places for play?

Each year children are injured or killed while trespassing on railroad property. Sometimes they are hit by a train as they walk along the tracks. What else can happen?

145

Dumps and junk yards are dangerous places to play. Why?
What is the danger of old refrigerators and trunks that
are sometimes found in dumps?

146

A quarry is a place where stone is dug out for building purposes. It is often as deep as 100 feet or more. What dangers might there be in playing near a quarry?

147

Going into places like empty buildings is against the law and may be dangerous. What dangers might there be in broken windows, rotten stairs, broken railings, and the like?

148

What First Aid Should Be Given?

Do you know what *first aid* means? First aid is the care that is given immediately in case of injury.

Sometimes, if the injury is a small one, first aid of the right kind is the only care that is needed. Otherwise, first aid is the care given until a doctor takes over.

Maybe you already know a few things about first aid. Do you know, for example, what to do for a bruise?

Compare your ideas with the method suggested below.

Then read to find out what to do for small cuts and for burns without blisters.

Bruises

Put ice or cold cloths on the bruise at once to reduce swelling and to relieve the pain.

Small Cuts

First, wash the cut with soap and water.

Next put a sterilized bandage or a clean cloth over the cut.

Press down on the cut to stop the bleeding.

If the cut is large or deep, a doctor should take care of it as soon as possible.

Burns Without Blisters

For a *minor burn without blisters,* run cold water or put ice cubes on the burned area at once. Keep this treatment up until the pain is no longer felt.

If the burn is blistered or deep, or if covers a large area of the body, the person should be cared for by a doctor immediately.

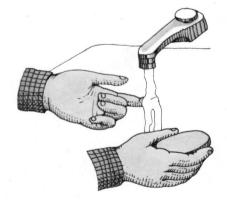

What steps do you see here for the treatment of cuts?

Check Yourself

1. Look back at the questions on page 124. How would you answer them now?

2. Why are empty houses unsafe places to play?

3. What are some dangers in playing on railroad property? Around a dump?

4. What is a jaywalker?

5. What are some dangers in playing around a quarry? Around construction work?

6. How can a pedestrian help keep himself safe at night?

7. On which side of the road should you ride a bicycle?

8. How is survival floating done?

9. What first-aid treatment should be given in case of a bruise? A small cut? A small burn without blisters?

10. What is missing from the following safety guide? *Look both ways before you cross a street.*

11. What should you be sure to wear if you go for a ride in a small boat?

12. How can you keep safe if you are walking with a group?

13. What have you learned about safety with ropes? With snowballs?

Things to Do

1. Make a safety study of your community. Look for safety aids such as signs, crosswalks, and overpasses. Look, too, for things that could be dangerous—things such as quarries and dumps. Later report to your class on what you have found in your study.

2. Think of some good safety guides for use with each of these:
   a. a chemistry set
   b. bows and arrows
   c. a skate board
   d. ice skates

3. Watch the headlines in your newspaper. Bring to class newspaper stories about accidents. Be ready to tell how the accidents might have been prevented.

4. Look at the safety posters shown on page 151. Can you answer the question above each poster?

5. Make a report on what to do in the event of an electric storm.

6. Do you think the use of alcoholic drinks might have anything to do with traffic accidents? See what you can find out about this and report your information to the class.

150

At what times should you be sure to follow the safety guide below?

What dangers does a jaywalker face in crossing streets?

Why do you need to wear white or carry a light when you walk at night or at dusk?

What important safety guide is given in the poster below?

Do You Remember the Safe Thing to Do?

For many years you have been learning about safe practices and about how to prevent accidents. Check yourself with the questions below to see how many important things you remember.

1. Suppose your clothes should catch fire. What would you do to put out the fire?

2. What are some safe things to do during a fire drill at school?

3. What are some safety ideas to keep in mind when you go on a trip with your class?

4. What should you do if a stranger should ask you to go with him or to take a ride in his car?

5. What are some safety precautions to follow when you go for a ride in a car?

6. What does the sign *No Trespassing* mean?

7. What should you be sure to do before you get in the bathtub or shower? Why?

8. What are some safety suggestions for swimmers?

9. What are some safety guides for bicycle riders to follow?

10. What should you do in case of fire at home?

11. What are the only safe places for crossing a street?

12. What should you do if a strange dog comes running toward you and growls at you?

13. What are some safety signs you see in your neighborhood every day?

14. What are some safety suggestions for bus riders?

15. What things will you look for in making a safety check on your bicycle?

16. What danger is there in playing in old refrigerators, chests, or other containers that can become airtight?

17. What signal does a bicycle rider give for a right turn? Left turn? Stop?

18. What have you done so far today to help keep yourself safe?

Self-Help Review

Use a ruler or a strip of paper to cover the answer column at the right. Read the first item and write the missing word or words on a piece of paper. Then move your ruler or paper strip down to uncover the answer and see if you are right. Go on in the same way with each of the other items. Do not write in this book.

The numbers by the answers show the pages in this book that give information about the subject. For the items you miss, go back and review this information.

1. When you walk on a road, walk to the _____.

left 126

2. When you walk at night or dusk, wear something _____ or carry a _____.

white
light 126

3. When picking string for a kite, pick a string without _____ on it.

metal 132

4. When you play softball, do not _____ the bat.

throw 134

5. Never _____ a gun at anyone.

point 136

6. When you put a cord into an electric socket, use the _____.

handle 138

7. If you ever have difficulty when you are swimming, try to use _____ _____.

survival
floating 141

Health Test for Unit Six

Part I

Write on your paper the number of each of the questions below. Copy each sentence and fill in the word or words needed to make a correct safety suggestion.

1. Use kite strings that do not have any _____ on them; do not fly kites in _____ weather.

2. Dead branches of trees are not _____ to climb on.

3. When you cross a street, cross at the _____ or in a _____.

4. If there is no sidewalk, walk so that you face the oncoming _____.

5. It is against the law to play in _____ houses.

6. Arrows and darts should always have _____ tips.

7. When you pull an electric cord from a socket, use the _____ of the cord.

8. When you are coming down a hill, you should _____ down, not run.

9. Be careful not to _____ the bat after you have hit a ball.

10. Be sure to _____ the turn if you plan to catch a pop fly in softball.

Part II

Copy each number on a piece of paper. After the number write the correct answer, *true* or *false*.

11. If you have a small cut, you should wash it with soap and water.

12. Railroad property is a safe place in which to play.

13. Before you cross a street, look to the left, look to the right, and then look behind you for turning cars.

14. You should put cold water on a bruise.

15. Airtight places or places that could become airtight are dangerous places to play.

16. You should have dry hands when you use electric equipment.

17. You can learn to keep yourself afloat in water for long periods of time.

18. Black is the safest color for bicycle riders at dusk.

19. It is unsafe to play around city dumps and junkyards.

20. Parking lots full of cars are safe play places.

Number of Answers   20

Number Right   _____

Score (Number Right × 5)   _____

7 What Helps Keep You From "Catching" Diseases?

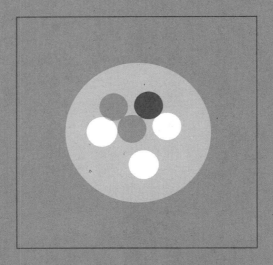

Diseases that can be "caught," or passed from one person to another, are called *communicable diseases*. Do you know how they are caused? Do you know how they differ from *noncommunicable diseases*? And do you know how the body tries to defend itself against diseases? Are there ways in which you become immune to some communicable diseases? These are some of the things you will find out in this unit.

Read to Find Out

1. *How do you get a communicable disease?*

2. *What are some ways in which you can pass along a communicable disease to others?*

3. *What are three main groups of disease germs?*

4. *How does your body try to fight off disease germs?*

5. *What important protective work is done by the white blood cells?*

6. *What are* antibodies *and how do they help you?*

7. *If you have had chickenpox once, are you likely to get it again? Explain.*

8. *How can vaccines help keep you from getting certain communicable diseases?*

9. *What is a* booster *dose or shot?*

What Is a Communicable Disease?

No doubt you have at times been ill with a cold. In a few days someone else in your family may have come down with a cold, too. And the other person may have said that he "caught" the cold from you.

How does one person "catch" an illness from another person? This happens only with the kind of diseases that are known as *communicable diseases.* Communicable diseases are always caused by tiny living plants and animals known as microbes, or *microörganisms.* The microörganisms that cause disease are called *germs.*

Something to Do
Look in your school or public library for books like these about microbes:
Lewis, Lucia Z. The First Book of Microbes *(Watts).*
Lietz, Gerald S. Junior Science Book of Bacteria *(Garrard).*
Selsam, Millicent E. Microbes at Work *(Morrow).*

Except when they are in large groups, germs are invisible to the naked eye. They can be seen only with the aid of a microscope. Disease germs produce such illnesses as diphtheria, whooping cough, mumps, polio, colds, flu, measles, chickenpox, typhoid, smallpox, and dysentery. What disease germs do you see pictured at the right?

Each disease is caused by its particular kind of germ. The germ that causes mumps causes mumps only; the germ that causes chickenpox causes just that disease and no other.

A person who is ill with a communicable disease has the germs of that disease in his body. For example, if the person has measles, he has measles germs in his body. The germs can be passed from a person sick with measles to a well person. Likewise, a person with a cold may pass the germs of the cold along to others; the germs are in the tiny droplets that come out of his mouth or nose as he talks, coughs, or sneezes.

There are some diseases, though, that are not caused by disease germs and that cannot be passed from one person to another. These diseases are called *noncommunicable diseases.* Such diseases are caused by some difficulty that occurs within the body itself.

Diabetes, for example, is a disease in which the body cannot properly use the sugar and starch in the diet. Diabetes is not a communicable disease. Nor is arthritis a communicable disease. When a person has arthritis, usually some of the body's joints become swollen and painful.

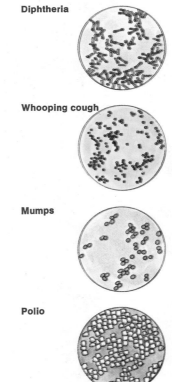

Diphtheria

Whooping cough

Mumps

Polio

Some microörganisms as seen under a microscope

What Are the Main Groups of Disease Germs?

You read about microörganisms on pages 77-79. You found out that some are helpful but a few of them are harmful. Some of the microörganisms that can cause disease are tiny one-celled plants; others are one-celled animals; still others are forms of viruses, which scientists still know little about.

Of these three main groups that cause disease, the one-celled plants called *bacteria* are the largest in actual size. The bacteria that cause disease are mainly of three shapes. Some are like tiny round balls; others are like straight rods; and still others are like spiral rods.

One-celled microörganisms of the animal world are called *protozoans.* Most of these are harmless. (Notice the picture of a harmless living protozoan on the cover of this book.) But some kinds of protozoans cause such diseases as amoebic dysentery, malaria, and sleeping sickness.

The third big group of disease germs, the *viruses,* are the tiniest germs of all. They are so tiny that a special microscope, called the *electron* microscope, has to be used to see them. The only kind of viruses now known about are harmful. Viruses cause such diseases as colds, flu, polio, measles, chickenpox, smallpox, mumps, and German measles.

All of these disease germs grow best in warm, moist places. Of course they thrive in the tissues of the human body. And once they are in the body, they begin to multiply at a very fast rate.

Protozoans

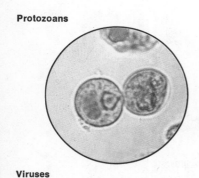

Viruses

Bacteria

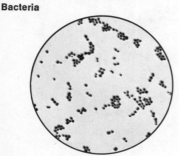

How Does the Body Fight Off Disease Germs?

Fortunately, many disease-causing germs never get very far into your body. They are kept out by the body's protective covering, the skin. If the skin is cut or broken, however, germs may enter through the opening.

What happens if germs *do* get into the body? Some of them enter the body with the air you breathe. But many of these germs are trapped, before they get any farther, by tiny hairs in your nose; still other germs are trapped in *mucus*. Mucus is a sticky fluid that keeps the lining of the nose and throat moist; it contains a germ-killing substance. Any germs that do succeed in reaching the lungs are likely to be coughed up. Most of the disease germs that come into your body with the food you eat are killed by saliva or stomach juices.

You have certain cells in your blood that can fight disease germs entering your body. There are two kinds of blood cells, red cells and white cells. It is the white cells that rush to fight off invading disease germs. Some of these white cells form a wall around the disease germs and keep them from spreading. Other white cells kill the germs by "eating" them. See the picture at the right.

Sometimes, though, the disease germs are not blocked off or killed by the white cells. Then the germs start to divide and grow and make more germs. Some of these germs produce substances that injure body cells or keep the cells from working properly. This causes you to get sick.

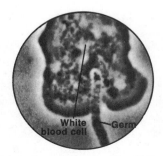

Notice the white blood cell "eating up" the germ.

In some cases, the growth of disease germs can be checked by medicines called *antibiotics*.

Antibodies

The body has still other ways of working against the germs that have entered the body and have made you sick. It can form *antibodies*. Antibodies are substances that circulate in the blood and that help white blood cells destroy germs.

The body makes a special kind of antibody to fight each kind of disease germ that enters it. After you get over the disease, some of these antibodies stay in your blood for a time—sometimes for many years and in some cases for a lifetime. If the germs of this same disease come into your body again, the antibodies are there to fight them off. For example, if you have had chickenpox, you are not likely to get it again. You have developed what is called *immunity* to that disease. You are immune because the antibodies built up during your first attack are able to kill off the chickenpox germs. For colds and flu, though, the period of immunity is *very* short.

Vaccines

Having a disease can be a dangerous way of building immunity to the disease. Fortunately, there is another way to prevent diseases in the body. Your body can be made to produce its own protection against different disease germs. Preparations such as *vaccines* can be injected into the body or can be given, as with polio vaccine, by mouth in syrup or in a lump of sugar. These vaccines cause your body to make antibodies.

160

Different vaccines contain different kinds of substances. Some vaccines are made of disease germs that have been killed. The vaccine against typhoid fever and the vaccine for whooping cough are of this kind. You are not harmed when these killed germs are injected into your body. What is more, your body reacts the same way to the killed germs as to the living ones. So if killed typhoid germs are injected, your body produces antibodies to fight off typhoid, without your getting sick. If killed whooping cough germs are injected, your body produces antibodies to fight whooping cough.

Some vaccines contain disease germs that are alive but greatly weakened. The smallpox vaccine and oral polio vaccine are of this kind. When the weakened germs enter your body, either they do not make you sick at all or they cause only a very mild illness. However, these germs do stimulate the body to make protective antibodies.

The protection given by a vaccine may not last as long as if you had the disease; therefore, it is usually necessary to have *booster* doses or shots.

One troublesome disease for which there is not as yet a truly successful vaccine is the common cold. It is hard for scientists to produce a cold vaccine because there are so many different kinds of cold germs infecting different body parts.

There *are* some vaccines, however, to immunize people against flu. Unlike other vaccines, these flu vaccines are not thought to be needed by children or by all adults but are given as recommended by a doctor.

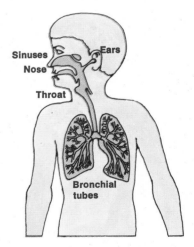

What areas of the body that are often affected by coldlike illnesses are shown above?

161

How Are Diseases Fought Around the World?

Every country in the world faces the problems of wiping out or controlling diseases of various kinds.

In the United States and in some other parts of the world, great progress has been made in learning how to fight diseases and to overcome poor sanitary conditions. New drugs and new kinds of medical equipment have been developed. And vaccines have been discovered to control many diseases. As a result, such diseases as malaria, yellow fever, scarlet fever, smallpox, tuberculosis, and diphtheria have been almost wiped out—or at least greatly reduced.

In other parts of the world, people are just beginning to learn how to fight off diseases. In these developing parts of the world, people want and need help. They need medical information, people to train health workers, modern vaccines, and the like.

Today many doctors, nurses, and public health workers are giving aid to those countries who need and want it. Some of these health workers come from an organization called the World Health Organization, or WHO. Some of the health workers are sent out by churches. A famous ship called HOPE sails into ports all over the world and health workers on it teach medical skills to the people.

On pages 163 to 169 you can see pictures of some of the different health activities that go on throughout the world.

Something to Do
Look in the library for information about the medical ship called HOPE.

These people in a Southeast Asian country are waiting their turn to see a doctor. The child in her mother's arms is suffering from smallpox.

163

This doctor has his "office" in the jungle. Sometimes a bench like the one you see here is the only place available for an examination of the patient.

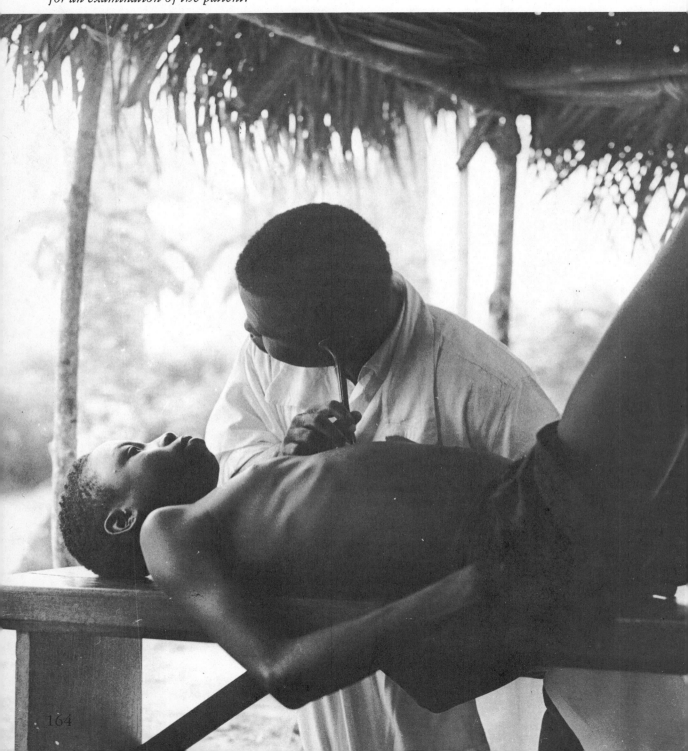

An elephant caravan makes up a malaria spray team in a developing country. Members of the team have to mount elephants to cross marshes and streams.

165

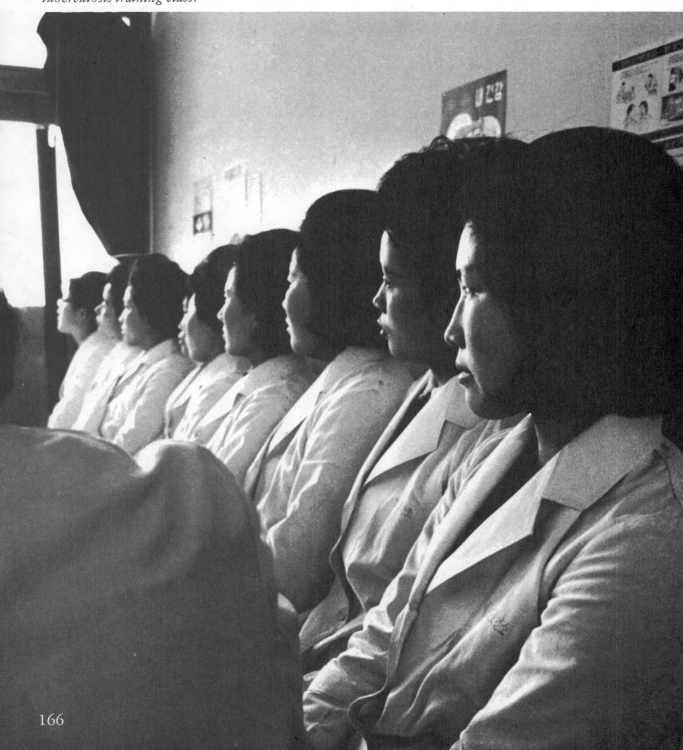

Many developing nations are making an all-out fight against tuberculosis. The nurses shown here are in a tuberculosis training class.

With freeze-dried vaccine, teams of doctors vaccinate children against smallpox. This disease is still a major killer in developing countries.

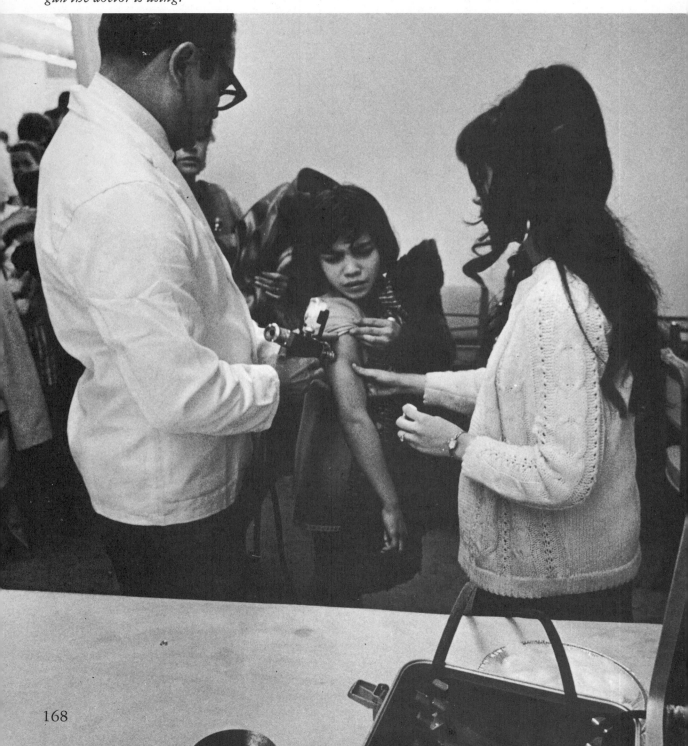

After an outbreak of diphtheria in Chicago a few years ago, a mass-inoculation program took place. Notice the jet-injector gun the doctor is using.

The two children here are studying health-education posters, issued by the government of a developing country. The posters have been put up on the village's one whitewashed wall.

1. Look back at the questions on page 156. How would you answer them now?

2. What is your explanation for each of these terms?

   a. antibodies

   b. communicable disease

   c. noncommunicable disease

   d. immunity

   e. microörganisms

   f. disease germs

   g. mucus

3. What is your explanation for this slogan? *Cover the sneeze, prevent disease.*

4. What are some important substances that vaccines have in them? What do these substances do?

5. Why is it difficult for scientists to make a vaccine that will keep you from getting the common cold?

6. Where are microbes found?

7. How many diseases can the whooping cough germ cause?

8. Is arthritis a communicable or a noncommunicable disease? Explain.

Things to Do

To find out if there are microbes on your fingers and in your coughs or sneezes, here is something to try.

Put three pieces of sliced, cooked potato on three small, clean saucers.

Have someone rub a finger over the potato on the first saucer. Label it.

Have someone cough on the potato on the second saucer. Label it.

Have someone sneeze on the potato on the third saucer. Label it.

Put each saucer in a clear plastic bag and seal it with tape.

Look at the potato slices every day.

How will you be able to see the microbes if they appear? They will be in large clumps containing millions of microbes and so you can see them.

Do not uncover the dishes at any time. Why?

Special Research

Prepare a report about a noncommunicable disease such as *lung cancer* or *chronic bronchitis* or *emphysema*. Be sure to tell what cigarette smoking may have to do with these diseases.

Use a ruler or a strip of paper to cover the answer column at the right. Read the first item and write the missing word or words on a piece of paper. Then move your ruler or paper strip down to uncover the answer and see if you are right. Go on in the same way with each of the other items. Do not write in this book.

The numbers by the answers show the pages in this book that give information about the subject. For the items you miss, go back and review this information.

1. Communicable diseases are the kind that are caused by _____ _____ .

disease germs 156

2. A disease that cannot be passed from one person to another is a _____ disease.

noncommunicable 157

3. The kinds of germs known as _____ are so small they can be seen only with an electron microscope.

viruses 158

4. The blood cells that fight off disease germs are the _____ cells.

white 159

5. When disease germs settle down in your body and begin to grow rapidly, you soon become _____ .

sick (or ill) 159

6. Vaccines are injected into the body to make it form _____ to fight off disease germs.

antibodies 160

7. Some vaccines have _____ germs in them, and some vaccines have _____ germs in them.

killed (or dead), weakened 161

8. After you have been given a certain vaccine, it may be necessary from time to time to have _____ doses or shots of it.

booster 161

Copy each number on a piece of paper. After the number write the letter that goes with the *best* answer choice.

1. The kind of germ that causes whooping cough
   a. causes other diseases, too
   b. causes that disease only
   c. causes polio as well

2. A communicable disease is always caused by
   a. mucus
   b. vaccines
   c. disease germs

3. Some common kinds of microbes are
   a. bacteria
   b. antibiotics
   c. antibodies

4. A noncommunicable disease is caused by
   a. disease germs
   b. a difficulty within the body
   c. a vaccine

5. The cells in the blood that help fight off disease germs are the
   a. red blood cells
   b. white blood cells
   c. antibiotics

6. Substances that are produced by the body and that help white cells kill disease germs are known as
   a. antibodies
   b. antibiotics
   c. immunities

7. Vaccines are useful because they cause your body to make protective
   a. mucus
   b. droplets
   c. antibodies

8. Three main groups of germs that cause diseases are
   a. anemia, diabetes, and flu
   b. bacteria, protozoans, and viruses
   c. measles, mumps, and polio

9. Microbes are found
   a. everywhere in the world around you
   b. chiefly in the human body
   c. only in the air

10. Disease germs that come into the body are
    a. usually harmless
    b. helpful
    c. harmful

Number of Answers   __10__

Number Right   _____

Score (Number Right × 10)   _____

8 What Are Some Community Health Problems?

Your community does many things to protect your health that you and your family cannot do for yourselves. What is more, new problems are arising that your community must think about and try to solve. Do you know what some of these important community health problems are? You will learn more about them in this unit.

Read to Find Out

1. *What is air pollution and why is it dangerous?*

2. *What causes water pollution and what can be done about it?*

3. *How is the community's food safeguarded?*

4. *In what ways may housing be a community health problem?*

5. *Can too much noise be a health problem? How?*

6. *What are some important things a health department does?*

What Do You Need to Stay Alive?

What are some things you must have if you are to stay alive and well? You need air to breathe, water to drink, food to eat, and housing to shelter you.

But if you are to stay as healthy as possible, just any air and water and food and housing will not do. You need clean air to breathe, pure water to drink, food that is safe to eat, and housing that meets your family's needs. And you and your family cannot get all these things by yourselves. You need the help of your community.

A most important job that your community faces is how to solve the problems that affect your health—problems of air and water pollution, unsafe food, and poor housing. Noise, litter, and signs of various kinds are also becoming very troublesome community health problems.

Something to Do
Look in the school or public library for such books as these:
Perera, Thomas B., and Orlowsky, Wallace. Who Will Wash the River? *(Coward).*

Peterson, Ottis. Junior Science Book of Water *(Garrard).*

Pringle, Laurence P. The Only Earth We Have *(Macmillan).*

Schneider, Herman and Nina. Let's Look Under the City *(Young Scott).*

Where Does a Community Get Its Water?

You must have water to drink and for other purposes, too. Your community tries to see that you get this water and that it is safe to use.

Many communities pipe their water in from nearby lakes and rivers. Sometimes a community gets water from deep-drilled wells. There are communities, too, that pipe their water in from storage places, or *reservoirs,* a hundred miles or more away. The large pipes that bring water to communities are called *water mains.* The water mains carry water first to the community *water-treatment plant.* Here it is treated with chemicals such as *chlorine* to kill harmful germs. The water is filtered through sand and gravel to remove dirt from it, and then it is sprayed into the air to further purify it.

How does water get from a water-treatment plant to buildings in the community?

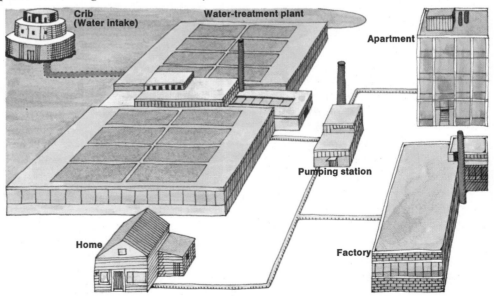

175

After water has been made safe for use, some of it is stored in large tanks. Much of it is piped to homes and other buildings in the community.

How Water Is Polluted

Water pollution is caused mainly by the dumping of wastes into rivers, lakes, and other bodies of water. From where do these wastes come?

Every time you open the drain in your sink or washbowl or bathtub, you send used water down a waste pipe and into sewer pipes. Wastes from garbage disposals and toilets are sent down waste pipes into sewer pipes, too. All these liquids and wastes are called *sewage.*

Most communities have sewer pipes underground to receive the wastes from homes and other buildings. In some communities these household wastes are carried through sewer pipes and dumped *untreated* into nearby lakes or rivers or streams.

Industries, too, may pollute water with their liquids and wastes. Harmful wastes may also drain off fields that have been sprayed with pesticides to kill harmful insects and weeds.

What Is Being Done About Water Pollution

You can see why water pollution should be prevented. Polluted water often has to be used for drinking. Even a modern water-treatment plant can have trouble purifying heavily polluted water.

Then, too, polluted waters are unpleasant and unsafe to have in a community. Fish may die in such waters. People can no longer swim in them. Polluted water often looks and smells bad. (See the pictures on pages 187-189.)

Special Research
1. Are there any lakes or rivers or streams in your community that are being polluted? In what ways are they being polluted? What is being done about this pollution? Can detergents be a pollution problem?
2. Are wastes being dumped that raise the temperature of nearby waters (thermal wastes)? How do you think these wastes affect fish?
3. Find out whether or not your community has a waste-treatment plant. If so, where is it located?

176

Water pollution can be reduced by the use of *waste-treatment plants.* Sewage can be piped to these plants to be made harmless *before* it is dumped into nearby waters. As yet, unfortunately, not all communities have such plants.

At the waste-treatment plant, solid materials and harmful bacteria are removed from the sewage. Chemicals are used to kill disease germs.

Industries can help reduce pollution by treating their wastes before dumping these wastes into nearby lakes, rivers, or streams. Ways must be found, too, to control use of dangerous pesticides that drain from fields into nearby waters.

The Federal government aids communities trying to solve their water-pollution problems by helping pay for research and for the building of waste-treatment plants.

How does sewage get to the sewage-treatment plant from its sources?

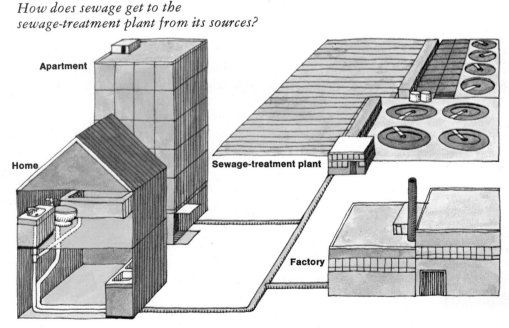

Apartment

Home

Sewage-treatment plant

Factory

How Can Food Be Polluted?

Food, like air and water, can also be polluted, or contaminated, and be a source of disease in the community. The germs of a great many common diseases are transmitted through food and milk.

How might the food and milk that you buy at stores or at restaurants in your community become a health hazard?

Food and milk, and the utensils they are served in, can easily be contaminated by cooks, waiters, or other food-service people who handle them with unclean hands or who use other unsanitary practices. Disease germs can get into food in all these ways and be passed along to people who eat it.

Rats, mice, flies, and cockroaches in unclean stores or restaurants may get into foods and spread dirt and germs there.

Foods can also be polluted by dirty storage places or unclean dishes.

Unsanitary food-handlers, careless dairy workers, and dirty milk containers can pollute milk before it gets to the dairy. That is why milk is *pasteurized,* or made pure, at the dairy, before it goes into stores to be sold.

People who are sick should not work where food is being prepared or served, or where dishes are being washed.

What Is Being Done About Food Pollution

One of the tasks of your community is to see that foods at food stores and restaurants are clean and safe for you to use. How is this done?

Something to Find Out
What is the pasteurization process? If you do not know, look up pasteurization *in the Glossary.*

178

There are health workers in your community and in your state who check to see that food stores and restaurants use sanitary methods of food-handling and food storage.

Food inspectors visit food stores and restaurants to see that the workers are clean. A check is made, too, to see that the surroundings are clean. The inspectors look at the floors, shelves, refrigerators, storage places, and washrooms.

If necessary, the inspectors teach the workers the important guides for food-handlers.

Some Guides for Food-Handlers

Below are some guides that inspectors stress with food-service workers. Why is each one important?

1. Before handling food, and right after using a handkerchief or going to the toilet, always wash your hands with soap and hot water and dry them on a clean towel, preferably a paper towel.

2. Avoid preparing or handling food if you have a cold, sore throat, or other illness—and if you have sores or cuts on your hands, arms, or face.

3. Keep all leftover foods that spoil easily at 45° F., or below, when they are stored.

4. In handling clean dishes, be sure fingers do not touch the inside surfaces of cups and glasses— or bowls of spoons, tines of forks, or knife blades.

5. Wash dishes, silverware, glasses, and all cooking utensils in plenty of hot, soapy water. Change dish water often. Rinse dishes with boiling water.

6. Use cups and plates that are free of breaks, cracks, or chipped places on any surfaces with which food comes in contact.

Did You Know?
In many communities, food stores and restaurants are given licenses to operate only if they have been inspected and found sanitary. Look in food stores and restaurants in your community to see if any such licenses are posted.

179

What Is Air Pollution?

When the air people breathe is polluted, this becomes a health concern of the community. The problem of air pollution is especially critical in cities. But it is becoming serious everywhere.

How does air become polluted? This can happen in many ways. Can you think of some of them?

Did you know that cars can pollute the air? In fact, cars, trucks, and buses are among the worst offenders. They cause pollution by sending into the air partly burned gases from their exhausts. Air pollution is caused, too, by smoke from the exhausts of jet planes on take-off.

Air is also contaminated by smoke from the burning of trash, by smoke from factories and homes, and by gases produced by some factories.

Dirt and smoke and gases that are poured into the air may be carried upward and away from us by wind and by air currents. But sometimes the air is quite still. Then smoke and gases are trapped near the earth, particularly in a low valley—and a blanket of what is called *smog* settles down over us. This smog is harmful, especially when it lasts for several days. (See the pictures on pages 190 and 191.)

Has your community ever been blanketed by smog? Did you cough? Did your eyes burn?

How Air Pollution Is Harmful

Look again at the pictures on pages 190 and 191 of smog in a large city. Think of all the ways you can why smog such as this might be harmful to people's health and safety and to property.

Something to Do
1. Tell why you think air pollution is most common in large cities.
2. Look for books like this one at your school or public library: Chester, Michael. Let's Go to Stop Air Pollution *(Putnam).*

180

Smog, as you may have decided, can irritate the eyes, nose, throat, and lungs. It can keep people from seeing as clearly as they should outdoors. Thus it can be a cause of accidents.

Air can also be polluted without your being able to see the pollution. Some of the harmful gases that are poured into the air are invisible. You may not smell these gases either.

Year after year of breathing polluted air can cause changes in the lungs that keep the air sacs from working properly. There is evidence that polluted air can be a factor in causing, or making worse, certain respiratory diseases. Diseases such as *emphysema* and *bronchitis* may result, especially among older people. And everyone may feel uncomfortable and lacking in energy on days when the air is more polluted than usual.

What sources of air pollution are shown in this picture?

181

Air pollution can rot and soil clothes, rust metals, and discolor paint on houses. It can also damage plant life. It costs billions of dollars annually.

What Is Being Done About Air Pollution

Now that you know some of the causes of air pollution, can you think of some ways in which communities can work to prevent it?

Did you decide that one good way to cut down on air pollution is to stop the burning of rubbish? Today many communities do forbid the burning of rubbish or leaves. And, instead of burning garbage that is collected, many communities now bury it. In time, it is thought that machines will be used to change garbage into building materials.

Nowadays many industries in the community use devices to reduce the smoke, dust, or harmful gases coming from their smokestacks. And in years to come more frequent use of atomic power will help reduce industrial air pollution.

To some extent, the harmful gases poured into the air from the exhausts of cars are being eliminated by the use of *afterburners*. Afterburners destroy gases by thoroughly burning the *carbon* in gasoline. All new American-made cars are equipped with antipollution devices. Gasoline of a higher quality will also help reduce pollution.

In many communities there is equipment to check the air for pollution. See the picture at left.

Today communities are helped by their state government and by the Federal government in working to prevent polluted air. How can you find out what *your* community is doing?

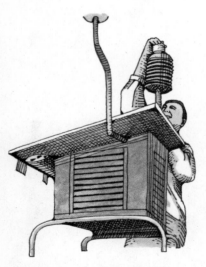

A jar covered with a sticky tape is placed on the top of this grey box. The sticky tape catches the dirty material in the air. Later, an examination of the tape will show the type of dirt that can be found in the air and also the direction from which the material came.

182

What Are Some Housing Problems?

In many communities, especially in large cities, there are not enough modern houses or apartments for people to live in. Some people have to live in old buildings that are crowded and unsanitary. At times several families may have to share one small apartment. Neighborhoods that are full of old, crowded, and unsafe buildings are called *slums*.

Many of the old buildings people must live in are not safe from fires. Some of the buildings have mice, fleas, and cockroaches in them; other buildings do not have any running water or toilets. Rats overrun slum buildings and are a hazard to health. They pollute food, spread disease germs, and may bite children. Most communities have programs to try to destroy rats by using poisons and rat traps. New buildings are being made so that they are ratproof.

Often these old houses and apartments are so close together that there are few yards and play places for the children to use. (See the picture of old buildings on page 192.)

An important job facing many communities is that of replacing these unsafe buildings.

In some cases the buildings may be torn down and replaced with new ones. In other cases, the old buildings may be completely repaired to make them safe and healthful dwellings.

Communities also need to encourage the building of low-cost houses for people to buy. (See the picture on page 193.)

What Do You Think?
Suppose you were an architect and could plan some new homes for people in a large city. Your homes would replace old ones that had been torn down. What plans would you make for safe and healthful places to live?

What About Noise and Other Problems?

Noise is all around us in our world today. Cars honk, brakes squeal, sirens scream, and trucks rumble along the streets. In some communities people work in factories where the machines are very noisy. And at airports some workers hear the roar of airplane engines all day long. Families who live near airports are also subjected to an unusual amount of noise.

Can you think of ways in which such noises in a community might annoy people? Do you think loud or high-pitched noises can damage health?

Some scientists have made studies showing that too much noise can be harmful to health. For one thing, living or working in places that are quite noisy can make some people nervous. Sleep may be disturbed. Noise may also cause some people to tire sooner than they would otherwise.

Studies have been made of workers who use loud machines in their work or who are employed in factories where noise levels are high. Many of these workers become hard of hearing, especially if they work around noise year after year.

One study of a group of people who live in New York City, which is very noisy, showed that high-pitched sounds had damaged their hearing to some extent. The people could no longer hear many high-pitched sounds around them.

Research indicates that listening to amplified music from rock bands can cause temporary hearing loss in the band members and the audience.

What Do You Think?
Too much noise can disturb the players in a game such as basketball. Can you give an example of how and when too much noise might disturb a basketball player?

184

Ways of Cutting Down on Noise

Many ways have been found to help reduce the noise in communities. Nowadays there are special materials that can be used to soundproof buildings. These materials are put on walls, windows, and ceilings. The materials keep indoor noises from being carried from room to room, and they keep outdoor noises from coming in.

Many machines have been made with motors that are less noisy than they once were. Today factories often put noisy machines in special soundproof rooms.

In many factories where it is not possible to cut down on loud noises, the workers are required to wear earmuffs and ear plugs.

In many homes, people are taking care to keep their radios and televisions from playing too loudly.

What sources of noise are shown in this picture?

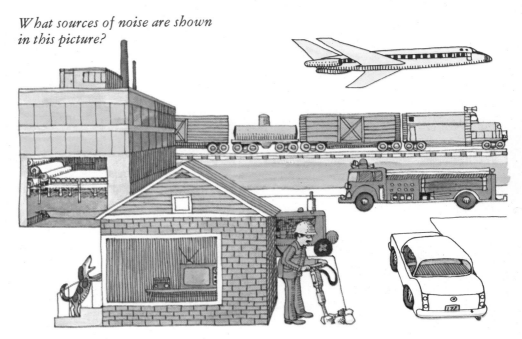

Some homes, schools, and offices have carpeting on the floors as a means of cutting down on noise.

Efforts are being made also to design railway and rapid-transit systems that will make less noise than they presently do. In many cases now there is less use of clanging bells and loud train whistles than formerly.

Much thought, too, is being given to how to muffle some of the noise made by jet planes. This could be done by installing sound-absorbent material around the engines.

Many communities now have passed laws to keep car drivers from honking horns too loudly. Other towns have laws that require noisy factories to close at night so that people's sleep will not be disturbed.

What are some of the noises that disturb people in your community?

What does *your* community do to lessen noise?

Community Eyesores

An excess of street and highway advertising signs is a matter of public concern. (Look at the picture on page 195.) Tell why jumbles of signs like these are sometimes called "community eyesores."

Dirt and litter on the streets are not only unsanitary, they can affect our feeling of order and well-being. In many communities it is against the law to carelessly drop old papers and trash on streets, in parks, and other public property. Do you think this is a good idea? Why or why not? (Look at the picture on page 196.)

Some Things to Do
1. Tell what you think is the difference between a sound *and a* noise. *Check your ideas with your dictionary.*
2. List all the ways you can in which noises can be made less noisy.
3. See if you can discover something that has been done in your *home or your school to reduce the noise. Then write about it.*

186

Pollution and Other Community Health Problems

*What do you think has caused the water pollution pictured here?
How else can water be polluted? What might be done about it?*

187

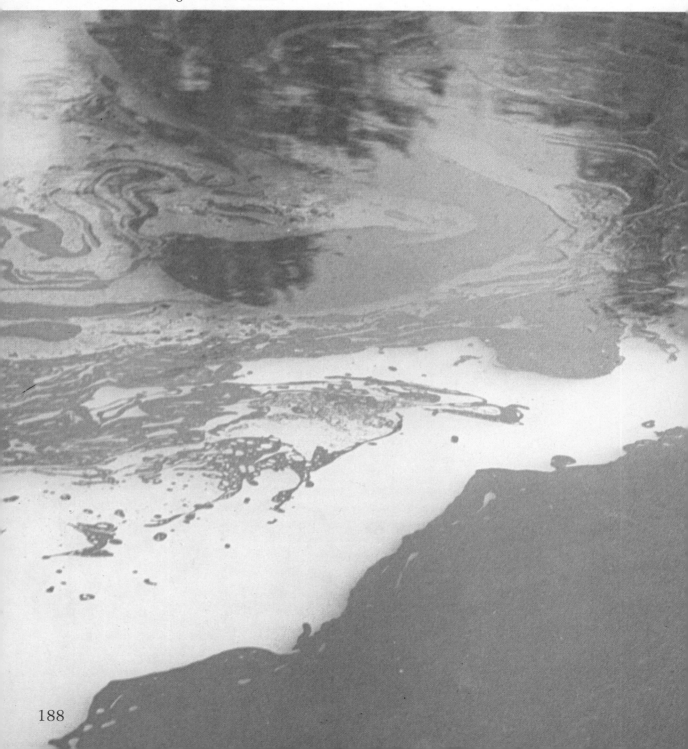

Oily material on the surface of water is called an "oil slick." From where might the oil come?

What has happened to these fish as a result of a polluted lake? What effects can this have on a community?

189

What can be done to prevent air pollution by factories in a community?

191

What are some of the health and safety problems that can grow out of slum apartments such as these?

This new apartment building has replaced a slum building.
What are some advantages of the new building?

193

What problems can be caused by all the traffic in a city?
What are some ways cities might lessen traffic problems?

The landscape here is being spoiled, or polluted. How?
What might be done about it?

195

Here you see another kind of pollution. What has caused it?
What can be done about it?

What About Drugs?

A problem that is becoming more and more a community-health problem concerns drugs. Drugs can, of course, be useful. A doctor may prescribe them to help the sick. People can buy nonprescription, or over-the-counter, drugs which, if used according to directions, may relieve headaches or the like.

But at times certain drugs are not used as directed by a doctor or by instructions on a package. In such cases, there could be many different reasons why people use them. Curiosity or to escape from problems are two reasons.

One drug that young people are sometimes tempted to use is marijuana, known as "grass" or "pot." Marijuana comes from the hemp plant. Parts of the hemp plant are crushed and rolled into cigarettes, often called "joints" or "Jays." Scientists are studying the long-term effects of marijuana on the body. It is known that marijuana can make a person feel confused or anxious and can affect his vision so that he misjudges distances. The use of marijuana is illegal. Possession of it is punishable by a fine or jail sentence.

Some drugs often misused are the "up-and-down drugs." The "up" drugs, sometimes called "pep pills," speed up the work of the nervous system; misuse of them can cause sleeplessness and shakiness. The "down" drugs slow down the work of the nervous system; misuse of them can cause breathing to be dangerously slowed down. People have died from an overdose of these drugs.

More Facts
1. Reactions to drugs are different in different people.
2. The "up" drugs are sometimes called "bennies," "A's," or "wake-ups." One of the "up" drugs is called "speed." Its use can cause some people to become violent.
3. The "down" drugs are often called "barbs," "reds and blues," or "goofballs." A person using such drugs without a doctor's prescription can easily take an overdose.
4. Glue, such as the plastic cement that comes in a tube, can also be misused. Continued deep sniffing of glue—or paint thinner, lighter fluid, gasoline, or the like—can cause damage to your brain, kidneys, liver, heart, and nervous system.

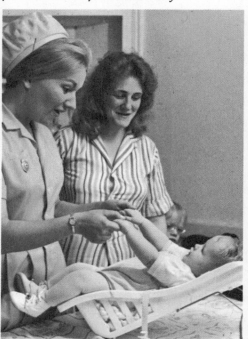

Public health nurses visit families and show them how to do such things as care for the sick or for a new baby.

Health-department laboratories test samples of public water supplies to be sure the water is safe for drinking.

What Does a Health Department Do?

Who is responsible in a community for improving public health conditions, for checking the spread of diseases, and for educating people about healthful ways of living?

You know, of course, that the families and the schools in a community are concerned with healthful living. But the chief responsibility for public health belongs to the health department.

Perhaps *you* have seen some examples of a public health department at work. What have you seen or heard about its work?

Some things other boys and girls your age have mentioned are shown in italics on page 199.

Local health departments coöperate with state and Federal authorities to inspect food and make sure it is prepared and sold under sanitary conditions.

Immunizations help prevent communicable diseases like smallpox, diphtheria, whooping cough, typhoid, polio, and measles.

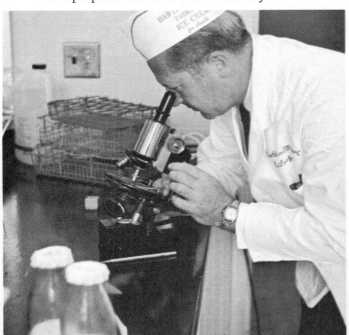 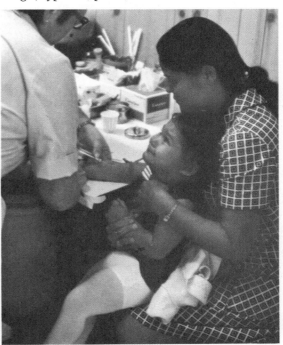

"Sometimes a nurse from the public health department comes to help a family where there is illness."

"We sometimes have special immunization drives."

"The health department has some pamphlets on health that people can get if they want them."

"In our community there is a well-baby clinic where mothers take their babies for health checkups."

Whether the health department is large or small, whether it is a city or a county department, the main services are the same. And working with the local health department are the state health department and the United States Public Health Service.

What does a health department do? What do the pictures on these two pages tell about their work?

Do You Know?
Does your community health department—or some other community group—do anything to help young people who have been unwisely experimenting with drugs? How can you find out?

199

Check Yourself

1. Look back at the questions on page 174. How would you answer them now?

2. When is a community likely to have smog settle over it? What are some harmful effects of smog?

3. How would you explain this statement, "Air pollution is expensive"?

4. Why do you think it is a good idea to wash fruits and vegetables before they are eaten raw?

5. How is the milk you drink made safe?

6. Why might a large city have more problems with air pollution than would a rural area?

7. What are some guides that those handling food should follow so they will not pollute foods they are preparing or serving?

8. Why are slums a community health problem? What can be done about them?

9. What are some effects of noise on a person's health?

10. What are some disadvantages to a community in having a polluted lake or river nearby?

11. What is the purpose of a community water-treatment plant?

Things to Do

1. Investigate—then list—the things your food store does to help keep the food clean and safe.

2. Tell about some things your community does to help keep people safe as well as healthy.

3. Write a paragraph or two about any one of these topics:

Why Air Pollution Is Dangerous

Why Noise Can Be a Problem

Why Drugs May Be Misused

How Drinking Water Is Made Safe

What a Food-Handler Should Know

Special Research

1. Water pollution is not the only problem some communities have. They may also be troubled by a *lack* of water. Find out what kind of research is being done to help solve the problem of water scarcity.

2. Investigate what, if anything, is done in your community to help people who may want to stop smoking—but who find it hard to stop the habit. Your school nurse may be able to help you.

Self-Help Review

Use a ruler or a strip of paper to cover the answer column at the right. Read the first item and write the missing word or words on a piece of paper. Then move your ruler or paper strip down to uncover the answer and see if you are right. Go on in the same way with each of the other items. Do not write in this book.

The numbers by the answers show the pages in this book that give information about the subject. For the items you miss, go back and review this information.

1. Another name for dirty air is _____ air.

polluted 180

2. Air can be polluted by _____ from the burning of fuel in houses and factories and by _____ from the exhausts of cars.

smoke
gases 180

3. Household wastes are called _____.

sewage 176

4. An important way to prevent water pollution is by the use of _____ _____ _____.

waste-treatment plants 177

5. Milk is _____ at the dairy to make it safe to drink.

pasteurized 178

6. Food-handlers should _____ their hands _____ preparing or serving food and _____ using the toilet.

wash, before after 179

7. A problem many communities face is that of replacing _____ buildings with safe, healthful buildings.

slum 183

8. Loud or high-pitched sounds can harm people's _____.

hearing 184

9. In many communities there is a _____ _____ that is responsible for community health problems.

health department 198

Health Test for Unit Eight

Part I

Copy each number on a piece of paper. After the number write the correct answer, *true* or *false.*

1. Smog is harmless.

2. Smoke can cause air pollution.

3. You can always see polluted air.

4. Air pollution can damage property.

5. In every truly healthful community, the garbage is burned in dumps.

6. Afterburners in cars can help do away with some air pollution.

7. It is safe to drink water dipped out of lakes or rivers.

8. Rivers and lakes can be polluted by having sewage dumped into them.

9. A waste-treatment plant can make sewage safe for dumping into nearby waters.

10. Polluted waters make safe, pleasant places for fishing and swimming.

11. Germs in food can spread diseases.

12. Poor housing is a health problem in a community.

13. Loud noises can harm the body.

14. Air pollution can cause accidents.

15. Food-handlers should avoid touching the inside surfaces of dishes.

Part II

Copy each number on a piece of paper. After the number write the letter that goes with the *best* answer choice.

16. Smog is most likely to occur
a. on a windy day
b. when the air is still
c. in villages or in the country

17. Air is polluted by
a. rain and snow
b. bright sunshine
c. smoke and gases

18. Lakes and rivers may be polluted by
a. noise
b. sewage
c. filtration

19. Foods that spoil easily should be kept in the
a. oven
b. refrigerator
c. cupboard

20. A health department usually has
a. public health nurses
b. reservoirs
c. slums

Number of Answers   20

Number Right   _____

Score (Number Right × 5)   _____

Review of Book

Page numbers after each question indicate pages in this book on which information about the question can be found, if it is needed.

<u>About the body and how it grows</u>

1. How does your body help control its temperature? (Page 9)

2. What causes you to feel hungry? (Page 10)

3. What happens to your body organs when you are asleep? (Page 12)

4. What are three ways in which the body helps protect itself? (Pages 8-16)

5. What reserve power does the body have? (Page 15)

6. What are some functions of the brain? (Page 16)

7. How does your skeleton help you? (Page 24)

8. What have you learned about growth patterns for children your age? (Pages 33-34)

<u>About food, teeth, and digestion</u>

9. What are two things that can help give you an appetite? (Pages 74-75)

10. What may happen if you eat a meal when you are feeling angry? (Page 76)

11. What can the right foods do for you? (Pages 56-57)

12. What are the four main food groups in the Food-for-Fitness guide? (Pages 60-61)

13. What are the parts of a tooth? (Page 88)

14. Why do you need teeth of different shapes? (Pages 90-91)

15. What is the main job your teeth have? What else do they do? (Page 92)

16. Why are permanent teeth sometimes out of place? (Page 103)

<u>About communicable disease and community health</u>

17. What is a communicable disease? (Page 156)

18. How does your body try to fight off communicable diseases? (Pages 158-161)

19. How do vaccines help in prevention of communicable diseases? (Pages 160-161)

20. Why is air pollution a health problem? (Pages 180-182)

21. What makes food spoil? (Pages 77-79)

22. What can be done about pollution of a community's water supply? (Pages 176-177)

End-of-Book Test

Part I

Write the number of each incomplete sentence below. After the number, write the word needed to finish the statement.

1. The hard white coat on the outside of a tooth is called_____.

2. The parts of the teeth found under the gums are the _____.

3. The four front teeth in the upper and lower jaws are called _____.

4. When you are in a very strong light, the pupils of your eyes become _____.

5. The sticky fluid in the nose and throat is called _____.

6. The air you breathe goes down into your lungs through the _____.

7. Each of the main senses has a place in the _____ where its messages are received and acted upon if necessary.

8. The bones of the _____ help protect your brain.

9. The cells in your blood that help fight disease germs are the _____ blood cells.

10. When you are hungry, the muscles of your stomach come together, or _____.

11. After you have hit a ball with a bat, _____ the bat; do not throw it.

12. Avoid touching any electric equipment when you have _____ hands.

13. For a small burn, run _____ water over the burn.

14. A disease that can be passed from one person to another is known as a _____ disease.

15. Materials that the body manufactures especially to fight off disease germs are called _____.

16. Communicable diseases are diseases caused by tiny living plants and animals known as _____.

17. Air that is unclean or dirty is called _____ air.

18. Wastes from garbage disposals and toilets are known as _____.

19. The best time to brush the teeth is right _____ eating.

20. Diseases that cannot be passed from one person to another are called _____ diseases.

Number of Answers	20
Number Right	_____
Score (Number Right × 5)	_____

Part II

Copy each number from 1 to 25 on your paper. Following each number, write *true* if the statement is true, write *false* if the statement is false.

1. All microbes are harmful.

2. Your body can fight germs.

3. Microbes divide to make more microbes.

4. The best time to brush your teeth is right before you eat.

5. Milk is frozen to pasteurize it.

6. Air pollution can be harmful to property in a community.

7. The best thing to do with garbage in a community is to ignore it.

8. Smog can be harmful to health.

9. Loud noises are never harmful to people's health.

10. The red blood cells help fight off disease germs.

11. Measles germs can also cause mumps.

12. Chlorine can be used to help purify water, or make it clean.

13. Air pollution can be a factor in causing diseases of the lungs.

14. As the air is passed through your nose, it is cooled.

15. Human beings are warm-blooded.

16. During strenuous exercise, the heart slows down its work of pumping blood through the body.

17. The body breathes in air without your having to think about it.

18. Normal body temperature is about 98.6° F.

19. Sleep gives the body a chance to renew itself.

20. A person can live with only one lung.

21. Every nine-year-old girl should weigh 80 pounds.

22. During all the growing-up years, boys are taller than girls of the same age.

23. Most boys do not grow much after they are twelve years old.

24. Foods give you energy.

25. Microbes can get into foods and spoil them.

Number of Answers	25
Number Right	_____
Score (Number Right × 4)	_____

Books of Information

Chester, Michael. *Let's Go to Stop Air Pollution* (Putnam). In this book you are shown an air-pollution control laboratory.

Frahm, Anne. *The True Book of Bacteria* (Childrens Press). Many interesting facts are given about bacteria.

Houser, Norman W. *About You and Smoking* (Scott, Foresman). This paperback gives you up-to-date facts on smoking and health.

McDonald, Barbara Guthrie. *Casserole Cooking Fun* (Walck). Easy, step-by-step directions are given for making casseroles.

Madison, Arnold. *Drugs and You* (Messner). A good "first" book on drugs.

Pringle, Laurence P. *The Only Earth We Have* (Macmillan). You can learn about the need for clean air and water—and the need to protect natural resources.

Ravielli, Anthony. *Wonders of the Human Body* (Viking). This book shows the body as the most perfect of all machines.

Schneider, Herman and Nina. *How Your Body Works* (Young Scott). Many questions about the body are answered in this book.

Showers, Paul. *A Drop of Blood* (Crowell). This story shows why blood is so important to us.

Books to "Grow On"

Calhoun, Katie. *Katie John* (Harper). A lonely girl has to adjust to a new home.

De Angeli, Marguerite. *Copper-Toed Boots* (Doubleday). Shad yearns for—and finally earns—a special pair of boots.

Hamilton, Virginia. *Zeely* (Macmillan). A city child grows up a little during a farm visit.

Konigsburg, Elaine L. *Altogether, One at a Time* (Atheneum). This book has four stories that deal with children's emotions.

Little, Jean. *From Anna* (Harper). Anna's secret is discovered; she cannot see well. Glasses and a special class help.

Madian, Jon. *Beautiful Junk* (Little, Brown). A curious boy sees a junk-created marvel.

Shotwell, Louisa R. *Roosevelt Grady* (World). The son of migrant farm workers longs for a real home.

Speevack, Yetta. *The Spider Plant* (Atheneum). A girl from Puerto Rico learns to adjust to apartment-house living.

Stolz, Mary. *A Wonderful, Terrible Time* (Harper). Two city girls get a chance to go to a summer camp. The title tells their reactions to the experience.

White, E. B. *Charlotte's Web* (Harper). This story has an unusual "cast of characters" who all understand the meaning of love.

Glossary

Full Pronunciation Key

The pronunciation of each word is shown just after the word, in this way: **ab bre vi ate** (ə brē′vē āt). The letters and signs used are pronounced as in the words at the right. The mark ′ is placed after a syllable with primary or heavy accent, as in the example above. The mark ′ after a syllable shows a secondary or lighter accent, as in **ab bre vi a tion** (ə brē′vē ā′shən).

Foreign Sound: н as in German ach. Pronounce k without closing the breath passage.

a	hat, cap	o	hot, rock
ā	age, face	ō	open, go
ä	father, far	ô	order, all
		oi	oil, voice
b	bad, rob	ou	house, out
ch	child, much		
d	did, red	p	paper, cup
		r	run, try
e	let, best	s	say, yes
ē	equal, be	sh	she, rush
ėr	term, learn	t	tell, it
		th	thin, both
f	fat, if	тн	then, smooth
g	go, bag		
h	he, how	u	cup, butter
		u̇	full, put
i	it, pin	ü	rule, move
ī	ice, five		
		v	very, save
j	jam, enjoy	w	will, woman
k	kind, seek	y	young, yet
l	land, coal	z	zero, breeze
m	me, am	zh	measure, seizure
n	no, in		
ng	long, bring		

ə represents:
a in about
e in taken
i in April
o in lemon
u in circus

ər represents:
er in mother
ur in pursuit

This pronunciation key is from *Thorndike-Barnhart Beginning Dictionary* (Scott, Foresman and Company).

ab scess (ab'ses), a collection of pus in some part of the body. An abscess results from an infection and is usually painful: *an abscess of a tooth.*

ac ci dent (ak'sə dənt), 1. an event not wanted, intended, or planned to happen, such as the dropping of a dish, a fall from tripping over something in the dark, or the colliding of two automobiles. 2. chance: *I cut my foot by accident.*

ac id (as'id), 1. sour; sharp or biting to the taste: *Lemons are an acid fruit.* 2. a chemical substance. The acids caused by fermentation of sweet foods in the mouth can cause tooth decay if these foods are not removed by brushing the teeth.

af ter bur ner (af'tər bər'nər), a burner attached to the tailpipe of a car that destroys gases by thoroughly burning the carbon in gasoline: *Afterburners are antipollution devices.*

an ti bi ot ic (an'ti bī ot'ik), chemical product of bacteria, yeast, and molds that destroys or weakens harmful microbes: *Penicillin is an antibiotic.*

an ti bod y (an'ti bod'ē), *pl.* **an ti bod ies,** substance produced in the blood of persons or animals that destroys or weakens bacteria or neutralizes poisons produced by them.

au to mat ic (ô'tə mat'ik), 1. moving or acting of itself: *an automatic lock, an automatic pump.* 2. done without thought or attention: *Breathing and swallowing are usually automatic.*

bac ter i a (bak tir'ē ə), tiny living plants that can usually be seen only through a microscope. Some bacteria cause disease and tooth decay; others cause milk to sour or turn cider into vinegar.

bi cus pid (bī kus'pid), tooth having two cusps, or pointed ends, that tears and grinds food. An adult has eight bicuspids.

blis ter (blis'tər), a little baglike place under the skin filled with watery matter. Blisters are often caused by burns or rubbing.

boost er dose (bü'stər dōs'), additional dose of a vaccine or serum given at stated intervals after the original dose or given as emergency treatment when exposure to a disease has occurred or is suspected.

brain (brān), the mass of nerve cells enclosed in the skull or head of a person or animal. The brain controls almost all of the functions of the body, and with it we can learn, think, and remember.

bron chi tis (brong kī'tis), inflammation of the mucous membrane that lines the bronchial tubes.

bruise (brüz), an injury to the body, caused by a fall or blow that breaks blood vessels without breaking the skin: *The bruise on my arm turned black and blue.*

caf feine or **caf fein** (kaf'ēn), a slightly bitter stimulating drug present in coffee and tea.

cal cu lus (kal'kyə ləs), *see* **tartar.**

cal o rie (kal'ə rē), 1. unit for measuring the amount of heat. 2. a unit of the energy supplied by food. An ounce of sugar will produce about a hundred calories.

can cer (kan'sər), harmful growth in the body that tends to spread and destroy healthy tissues and organs; a malignant tumor. There are many different kinds of cancer.

car bon di ox ide (kär′bən dī ok′sīd *or* dī ok′sid), a colorless, odorless gas present in air. It is a waste product formed by the body and is removed from the body by the lungs. You breathe out, or exhale, carbon dioxide that is in your lungs.

car ies (ker′ēz or kar′ēz), *see* **dental caries.**

cav i ty (kav′ə tē), *pl.* **cav i ties,** *see* **dental caries.**

ce men tum (sə men′təm), hard, thin substance covering the roots of a tooth up to its neck.

chlo rine (klôr′ēn′), a greenish-yellow gas, irritating to the nose and throat. Chlorine can kill certain disease germs.

clot (klot), 1. half-solid lump: *A clot of blood formed in the cut and stopped the bleeding.* 2. form into clots: *Milk clots when it becomes sour.*

cold-blooded (kōld′blud′id), having blood that is about as cold as the air or water around the animal. Reptiles are cold-blooded; birds and mammals are warm-blooded.

com mu ni ca ble dis ease (kə myü′nə kə bl də zēz′), disease which can be passed from person to person.

com pen sate (kom′pən sāt), to give something which makes up for a loss, injury, and so on: *Skill sometimes compensates for lack of strength.*

con nec tive tis sue (kə nek′tiv tish′ü), tissue made up of an interlaced mass of tough, elastic cells that connects, supports, or encloses other tissues and organs in the body.

con tam i nate (kən tam′ə nāt), defile; pollute; taint; corrupt: *Flies contaminate food.*

con tract (kən trakt′), draw together; make or become narrow; shorten; make or become smaller; shrink: *Muscles contract to help move bones.*

crown (kroun), part of a tooth which appears beyond the gum, or an artificial substitute for it.

cus pid (kus′pid), tooth having one cusp, or pointed end, and used especially for tearing food; there are four cuspids in a full set of teeth.

den tal car ies (den′tl ker′ēz or kar′ēz), destruction of dental tissues; tooth decay; cavity.

den tin (den′tin), hard, bony material beneath the enamel of teeth. It forms the main part of a tooth.

di gest (də jest′ or dī jest′), change (food) in the mouth, stomach, and intestines so that the body can use it: *We digest our food; the food is digested.*

diph ther i a (dif thir′ē ə or dip thir′ē ə), infectious disease of the nose and throat. People can be inoculated to prevent their catching diphtheria.

dis ease (də zēz′), 1. sickness; illness. 2. any particular illness: *Measles and chickenpox are two diseases of children.*

dis ease germ (də zēz′ jėrm′), microbe that causes disease.

dys en ter y (dis′ən ter′ē), a disease of the intestines, producing diarrhea with mucus and blood.

EEG, *see* **electroencephalogram.**

e lec tro en ceph a lo gram (i lek′trō en sef′ə lə gram), tracings of brain waves made by the electroencephalograph machine. *Abbrev:* EEG.

---

hat, āge, fär;   let, bē, tėrm;   it, īce;   hot, gō, ôrder;   oil, out;   cup, pùt, rüle;   takən, mothər

e lec tron mi cro scope (i lek′tron mī′krə skōp), microscope that uses beams of electrons rather than beams of light to enlarge images and that has much higher power than an ordinary light microscope.

em phy se ma (em′fə sē′mə), respiratory disease in which the air sacs become enlarged and inefficient in supplying oxygen to and removing carbon dioxide from the blood. Cigarette smoking can cause emphysema.

e nam el (i nam′l), the hard, white substance that covers and protects the crown of a tooth. Enamel cannot be regrown.

e rupt (i rupt′), burst forth: Teeth are said to erupt when they break through the gums.

e soph a gus (ē sof′ə gəs), tube for the passage of food from the mouth to the stomach.

e vap o rate (i vap′ə rāt′), 1. turn into vapor: *Boiling water evaporates rapidly.* 2. remove water from: *Heat is used to evaporate milk.* 3. give off moisture.

ex ca va tion (eks′ kə vā′shən), 1. a digging out; digging. 2. hole made by digging.

ex tract (eks trakt′), pull out or draw out, usually with some effort: *extract a tooth.*

F., an abbreviation for Fahrenheit.

Fahr en heit (far′ən hīt), on the Fahrenheit thermometer, 32 degrees is the temperature at which water freezes, and 212 degrees is the temperature at which water boils.

flu o resce (flü′ə res′), to give off light or glow from X-ray or ultraviolet radiation.

fluor i da tion (flur′ə dā′shən), process of adding small amounts of a fluoride to drinking water. Fluoridation of the water helps prevent tooth decay.

flu o ride (flü′ə rīd′), fluorine compound that may be added to drinking water in small amounts or applied directly to the teeth by a dentist to help prevent tooth decay.

flu o rom e ter (flu′ə rom′ə tər), a device that measures the fluorescence or glow that is given off by an object under examination.

freeze-dry (frēz′ drī′), to dry by freezing and evaporating the moisture content in a vacuum. Freeze-dried substances keep well without being refrigerated.

germ (jėrm), a very tiny animal, plant, or other living organism which is too small to be seen without a microscope; a microbe. The microbes that cause disease are called germs: *the germs of pneumonia.*

gland (gland), organ in the body which makes and gives out some substance which helps the body do its work.

gly co gen (glī′kə jən), a starchlike substance by which excess sugar is stored in the body, largely in the liver but also in the muscles. It can be changed quickly back into sugar when needed by the body.

grav i ty pull (grav′ə tē pùl′), the natural force that causes objects to move or tend to move toward the center of the earth.

gum (gum), the firm flesh around the teeth.

health (helth), 1. a being well or not sick; freedom from sickness. 2. condition of the body: *good health, poor health.*

hep a ti tis (hep′ə tī′tis), inflammation of the liver.

im mune (i myün′), not susceptible; protected by inoculation: *Vaccination makes people immune to smallpox.*

im pur i ty (im pyür′ə tē), *pl.* **im pur i ties,** 1. something that is dirty, filthy, or unclean. 2 thing that makes something else impure: *Filtering the water removed some of its impurities.*

in ci sor (in sī′zər), tooth having a sharp edge for cutting; one of the front teeth. An adult has eight incisors.

in sec ti cide (in sek′tə sīd), substance for killing insects.

i ris (ī′ris), the colored part of the eye around the pupil.

kid ney (kid′nē), one of the pair of organs, in mammals, birds, and reptiles, that takes waste matter and excess water from the blood and passes them off through the bladder in liquid form as urine.

large in tes tine (lärj′ in tes′tən), the lower part of the intestines into which the small intestine discharges food that has been digested.

liv er (liv′ər), the large, reddish-brown organ that makes bile, aids in the absorption of food, and stores certain food substances until they are needed by the body.

man di ble (man′də bəl), a jaw, especially the lower jaw.

mar i jua na or **mar i hua na** (mar′ə wä′nə), drug made from dried leaves and flowers of the hemp plant. It is a mild hallucinogen; it is dealt with legally as a narcotic.

mar row (mar′ō), the soft tissue that fills the hollow central part of most bones.

max il lar y (mak′sə ler′ə), of or having to do with the jaw, especially the upper jawbone.

mi crobe (mī′krōb), *see* **microörganism.**

mi cro ör gan ism (mī′krō ôr′gə niz′əm), an animal or plant organism too small to be seen except with a microscope. Germs are microörganisms.

mo lar (mō′lər), a tooth with a broad surface for grinding. A person's back teeth are molars.

mold (mōld), a microörganism of the plant kingdom that appears as a woolly or furry growth on food and other surfaces and is often black or greenish in color.

mo tor nerve (mō′tər nėrv′), bundle of nerve fibers that arouse muscles to action. When you want to walk or talk, motor nerves carry messages from the brain or spinal cord to the muscles.

mu cus (myü′kəs), a slimy substance that is secreted by and moistens the linings of the body. A cold in the head causes a discharge of mucus from the nose.

---

hat, āge, fär;   let, bē, tėrm;   it, īce;   hot, gō, ôrder;   oil, out;   cup, pùt, rüle;   takən, mothər

neck (nek), 1. part of the body that connects the head with the shoulders. 2. part of a tooth between the crown and the root.

non com mu ni ca ble dis ease (non'kə myü'nə kə bl də zēz'), disease that is not caused by disease germs and that cannot be passed from one person to another.

o cean og ra pher (ō'shə nog'rə fər), a specialist in oceanography, the science that deals with the ocean and its phenomena.

or tho don tist (ôr'thə don'tist), dentist who specializes in aligning teeth or moving them into proper position.

pas teur i za tion (pas'chər ə zā'shən), process of heating a substance to a high enough temperature to destroy harmful bacteria, and then chilling it quickly.

pe des tri an (pə des'trē ən), a person who goes on foot: *Pedestrians have to watch for automobiles turning corners.*

pen i cil lin (pen'ə sil'ən), antibiotic that is made from mold.

per i o don tal mem brane (per'ē ə don'tl mem'brān), soft covering surrounding a tooth and holding it in place in the jaw.

per ma nent teeth (pėr'mə nənt tēth'), the second set of teeth (of which there are 32), which start to come in when the primary teeth begin to come out. They are intended to last a lifetime.

per spi ra tion (pėr'spə rā'shən), sweat: *The runner's forehead was damp with perspiration.*

per spire (pər spīr'), to sweat.

phos phate (fos'fāt), a substance containing the chemical element phosphorous: *Phosphates are widely used in industry and agriculture.*

plate let (plāt'let), one of many small disks which float in the blood plasma.

pol lute (pə lüt'), make dirty; destroy the purity or cleanness of: *The water at the bathing beach was polluted by sewage from the city.*

pore (pôr), a very small opening. Sweat comes through the pores in the skin.

pos ture (pos'chər), position of the body; way of holding the body: *Good posture goes along with good health.*

pre serve (pri zėrv'), 1. keep from harm or change; keep safe; protect. 2. prepare (food) to keep it from spoiling. Boiling with sugar, salting, smoking, and pickling are different ways of preserving food.

pri mar y teeth (prī'mer'ē or prī'mə rē tēth'), the first set of teeth (of which there are 20), which are later replaced by the permanent teeth.

proc ess ing (pros'es ing), treating or preparing by some special method.

pro por tion (prə pôr'shən), 1. relation of two things in magnitude; a size, number, or amount compared to another. 2. proper relation between parts. 3. fit (one thing to another) so that they go together.

pro to zo ans (prō'tə zō'ənz), microscopic animals that consist of single cells.

pulp (pulp), the soft inner part of a tooth, containing blood vessels and nerves.

pu pil (pū′pl), opening in the center of the iris of the eye. It looks like a black spot. The pupil, which is the only place where light can enter the eye, expands and contracts, thus controlling the amount of light that strikes the retina.

pus (pus), a thick yellowish-white fluid formed in infected body tissues.

quar ry (kwôr′ē), *pl.* **quar ries,** place where stone is dug, cut, or blasted out for use, usually in building.

red blood cells (red′ blud′ selz′), cells that with the white blood cells form a large part of blood. Red blood cells contain a substance called hemoglobin, which gives them their color. Red blood cells carry oxygen from the lungs to various parts of the body.

re serve (ri zėrv′), anything that is kept back for future use: *Sleep helps renew a person's reserve of energy.*

root (rüt *or* rut), the part of a tooth that is covered by the gums and cannot be seen.

sa li va (sə lī′və), the liquid that the salivary glands secrete into the mouth to keep the mouth linings moist, to aid in chewing, and to start digestion.

sal i var y gland (sal′ə ver′ē gland′), any of the various glands that empty their secretions into the mouth.

san i tar y (san′ə ter′ē), 1. of or having to do with health; favorable to health; preventing disease. 2. free from dirt and filth.

scab (skab), the crust that forms over a sore or wound as it heals.

sca ler (skā′lər), an instrument for removing tartar, or calculus, from the teeth.

sen sor y nerve (sen′sər ē nėrv′), bundle of nerve fibers that carry messages from the sense organs to the brain. Pain, temperature, touch, sight, smell, sound, and taste are conveyed by sensory nerves.

set (set), put in the right place, position, or condition for use; arrange; put in proper order: *The doctor will set Dan's broken leg.*

sew age (sü′ij), the waste matter which passes through sewers.

skull (skul), the bony framework of the head.

slum (slum), a crowded, dirty part of a city.

small in tes tine (smôl′ in tes′tən), the long, winding tube which receives partly digested food from the stomach. The small intestine completes the digestion of the food and sends it into the blood.

smog (smog), a combination of smoke and fog in the air.

sound waves (sound′ wāvz′), waves set up by rapid movements of something to and fro; motion by which sounds are transmitted.

space main tain er (spās′ mān tān′ər), a temporary appliance inserted in place of a missing tooth to keep the teeth next to it from moving out of place.

---

spec i men (spes′ə mən), one of a group or class taken to show what the others are like; single part or thing regarded as an example of its kind: *A specimen of the tumor was examined.*

ster ile (ster′əl), free from living germs: *A doctor's operating instruments must be kept sterile.*

tar tar (tär′tər), a substance formed by the action of saliva on food which collects on the teeth and which must be removed by the dentist; calculus. Removal of tartar helps the dentist detect early signs of tooth decay.

tem per a ture (tem′pər ə chər), degree of heat or cold. The temperature of freezing water is 32° F. The normal body temperature is about 98.6° F.

tis sue (tish′ü), living substance forming some part of an animal or plant; a mass of similar cells which performs a particular function.

ty phoid fe ver (tī′foid fē′vər), an infectious disease characterized by intestinal inflammation, and caused by a germ taken into the body with food or drink.

ul tra vi o let rays (ul′trə vī′ə lit rāz′), the invisible rays in the part of the spectrum beyond the violet. They are present in sunlight, light from mercury-vapor lamps, and are important in healing, forming vitamins, and so on.

ur i nar y blad der (yùr′ə ner′ē blad′ər), a soft thin bag in the body that receives urine from the kidneys.

vac cine (vak′sēn′ *or* vak sēn′), substance containing weakened or killed virus or the killed bacteria of a particular disease that can be injected into the body or given orally to stimulate the body to produce antibodies.

vi rus (vī′rəs), any of a group of disease-producing microöganisms that reproduce only inside living cells and are too small to be seen through an ordinary microscope.

vi sion (vizh′ən), power of seeing; sense of sight: *The man wears glasses because his vision is poor.*

vol un tar y (vol′ən ter′i), 1. done, made, or given of one's own free will; not forced or compelled. 2. controlled by the will: *a voluntary action.*

warm-blood ed (wôrm′ blud′id), having blood that stays at about the same temperature regardless of the surrounding air or water. The temperature of warm-blooded animals is from 98 degrees to 112 degrees. Cats are warm-blooded; snakes are cold-blooded.

white blood cells (hwīt′ blud′ selz′), colorless cells that float in the blood and lymph. Some of them destroy disease germs.

wind pipe (wind′ pīp′), the passage by which air is carried from the throat to the lungs; the trachea.

yeast (yēst), the substance that causes bread dough to rise and beer to ferment. Yeast consists of very small fungi that grow quickly in a liquid containing sugar.

---

hat, āge, fär;   let, bē, tėrm;   it, īce;   hot, gō, ôrder;   oil, out;   cup, pùt, rüle;   takən, mothər

Index

About the Book

A Health Program for Nine- to Ten-Year-Olds

Book Four of the HEALTH AND GROWTH Program[1] is especially designed to meet the health needs, interests, and curiosities of children who are nine and ten years old.

Nine- to ten-year-olds have high interest in such things as how the body can protect itself, how the body grows, how germs can affect us, how we can help prevent communicable diseases, what new things are being learned about care of the teeth, and why it matters what kinds of food we eat. Information on such topics is provided in this text.

There is material, also, to satisfy boys' and girls' growing concern about community health and the environment (ecology). Such matters as air and water pollution, impure food, housing problems, and excessive noise are dealt with.

A strong strand of family-living material is woven into the unit entitled "How Do You Grow?" Here youngsters are helped to consider not only physical growth but emotional growth in such matters as becoming good family members.

The safety needs of nine- and ten-year-olds, whose work and play activities are expanding, are many and varied. *Book Four,* therefore, utilizes problem-solving situations to treat safety for pedestrians; safety in such activities as climbing and throwing; safety with guns; safety when swimming; safety in such games as softball; and safety around the home. The kinds of places that are never safe for play, such as city dumps, abandoned houses, and quarries, are discussed. Simple first-aid procedures are also included.

Children at this age are likely to be very much interested in sports and sportsmanship. And so a unit called "How Will You Play?" is included. Here boys and girls are helped to explore the many ways they can move their bodies and to consider how various ideas and emotions can be communicated by body movement. Directions for some ever popular games are provided, and there is an opportunity to think about the meaning of good sportsmanship.

An added feature of the book is the recurring appearance of boys' and girls' own health questions as revealed in classroom surveys. Among the questions asked by children themselves are these: *How does a cut heal? How does a broken bone mend? Do alcoholic drinks and tobacco hurt the body? What is wrong with eating in a hurry? Why are permanent teeth sometimes out of place?* Answers to these and many similar queries are given.

Throughout each unit, and at ends of units, meaningful activities and experiments are suggested. Also at the ends of units—and of the book—tests are furnished to help children check their progress in mastering important health concepts. Teaching suggestions appear throughout the *Teacher's Edition,* which includes overprinted "Teacher's Notes" and a special *Resource Book.*

The search for supplementary reading materials will be facilitated by the reading lists provided throughout the text, as well as at the close of the pupil's book and the *Resource Book.* Additional reading lists appear in the unit openings in the *Resource Book.*

Readability

Classroom tryouts of the text in prepublication form, as well as the use of various readability checks, indicate that *Book Four* is suitable for use with youngsters at the fourth-grade level.

---

[1] The HEALTH AND GROWTH Program includes *Off to a Good Start* (Junior Primer Activity Sheets), and *Book One* through *Book Eight,* with accompanying *Teachers' Editions.* Also available is a preprimary health program, *Health and Safety Highlights: Pictures and Songs for Young Children.*

Index of Health and Safety Ideas[1]

---

[1]Selected behavioral objectives for this level are given in the *Resource Book,* page 27.

223

Credits

Cover: Microphotograph by Dr. Roman Vishniac.
Unit 1: 8, 9, 11—Drawings by Lou Barlow, AMI. 12—Photographs courtesy of the Clinical Neurophysiology Laboratory of the Section of Neurology, University of Chicago. 13, 14, 15, 17-24, 25, 26—Drawings by Lou Barlow, AMI. 28—Drawings by George Suyeoka.
Unit 2: 32, 33—Drawings by George Suyeoka. 35-40—Photographs by Myles DeRussy. 36-39—Photographic charts on these pages are based on growth charts in Nancy Bayley's chapter "How Children Grow" in *The New Encyclopedia of Child Care and Guidance* edited by Sidonie Matsner Gruenberg. Copyright © 1954, 1956, 1959, 1963, 1967, 1968 by Doubleday & Company, Inc. Adapted by permission of the publisher. 42, 43, 44, 45, 46, 49, 50, 51—Drawings by George Suyeoka.
Unit 3: 57, 60, 61, 63, 64—Drawings by George Suyeoka. 65—Photograph by Stern-Foto Hopker from Black Star. 66—Photograph by Dick Swanson from Black Star. 67—Photograph by Paul Almasy, courtesy of the World Health Organization. 68-71—Photographs by Ralph Cowan. Products shown on these pages courtesy of Archer Daniels Midland Company, Minneapolis, Minnesota; Spreckles Sugar Company, Woodland, California; Worthington Foods, Inc., Worthington, Ohio. 72—Photograph by Archie Lieberman. 73—Drawing by George Suyeoka. 74, 75, 76—Drawings by Lou Barlow, AMI. 77—Photograph by James Ballard. 78, 80, 84—Drawings by George Suyeoka.
Unit 4: 88, 89, 90, 91, 93-95—Drawings by Lou Barlow, AMI. 96-97—Photographs by Lyle Mayer. 98—Photographs courtesy of Captain Gordon H. Rovelstad, United States Navy, Dental Research Institute, Naval Training Center, Great Lakes, Illinois. 99, 100, 101—Drawings by Lou Barlow, AMI. 102—Drawing by George Suyeoka. 103—Drawing by Lou Barlow, AMI.
Unit 5: 109, 110, 111, 112—Drawings by George Suyeoka. 113-116—Photographs by Ray Komorski. 121—Book cover from *Stilts, Somersaults, and Headstands: Games and Poems Based on a Painting by Peter Breughel.* Copyright © 1968 by Kathleen Fraser. Used by permission of Atheneum Publishers.
Unit 6: 125, 127, 129, 131, 133, 135, 137—Photographs by Michel Ditlove. 139—Photograph by Myles DeRussy. 140, 141—Drawings by George Suyeoka. 143-148—Photographs by Archie Lieberman. 149, 151—Drawings by George Suyeoka.
Unit 7: 157—Drawing by Lou Barlow, AMI. 158 (Top)—Courtesy of S. Stanley Schneierson, M.D., and Abbott Laboratories. 158 (Middle)—Courtesy of A. R. Taylor, Ph.D., Laboratory Director of Virus Research, Parke, Davis & Co. 158 (Bottom)—Courtesy of S. Stanley Schneierson, M.D., and Abbott Laboratories. 159—Photograph courtesy of Dr. James G. Hirsch, The Rockefeller University. 161—Drawing by Lou Barlow, AMI. 163—Photograph by Stern Foto Hopker from Black Star. 164—Photograph by Paul Almasy courtesy of the World Health Organization. 165—Photograph by P. N. Sharma, courtesy of the World Health Organization. 166—Photograph by Philip Boucas, courtesy of the World Health Organization. 167—Photograph by T. S. 'Satyan, courtesy of the World Health Organization. 168—Photograph by Arnold Zann. 169—Photograph by Marc Riboud, courtesy of the World Health Organization.
Unit 8: 175, 177, 181, 182, 185—Drawings by George Suyeoka. 187—Photograph by John Launois from Black Star. 188—Photograph courtesy of Environmental Protection Agency. 189—Photograph by Rhodes Patterson. 190—Photograph by Gerry Cranham from Rapho Guillumette. 191, 192—Photographs by John Launois from Black Star. 193, 194—Photographs by Joseph Sterling. 195-198, 199 (Top Left)—Photographs by Archie Lieberman. 199 (Top Right)—Photograph by Arnold Zann.

For coöperation in photographing situations on pages 35, 40—Timber Ridge School, Skokie, Illinois; on pages 113-116—St. Michael Grade School, Chicago, Illinois.

224